In this glossary:

[a] is pronounced as in f<u>a</u>r
[e] is pronounced as in g<u>e</u>t
[ee] is pronounced as in f<u>ee</u>t
[i] is pronounced as in s<u>i</u>t
[o] is pronounced as between g<u>o</u>t and g<u>oa</u>t
[oo] is pronounced as in l<u>oo</u>se
[y] is pronounced as in <u>y</u>es

Vuiko Yurko

The First Generation

By Danny Evanishen

Published by
Ethnic Enterprises
Publishing Division
Summerland, BC

Canadian Cataloguing in Publication Data

Evanishen, Danny, 1945-
  Vuiko Yurko

  ISBN 0-9697748-0-X

  1. Ukrainian Canadians--Fiction.* 2. Ukrainian Canadians--Humor* 3. Canadian wit and humor (English)* I. Title.
PS8559.V36V84 1994   C813'.54   C94-910221-0
PR9199.3.E92V84 1994

Ethnic Enterprises
Publishing Division
Box 234
Summerland, BC
V0H 1Z0

Printed and Bound in Canada
by New Horizon Printers
Summerland, BC

4 5 6 7 8 9 10 • 05 04 03 02 01 2000 99 98 97 96

Table of Contents

This book is dedicated to those who left their homes to come to a strange new land so that their children would have a better life.

Thank you, Baba and Dido.

Foreword

Canada has embraced a great many immigrants in her short history. Many Ukrainian people came to Canada over the years, and their history in this country is one of toil, sacrifice, homesickness, ill health, despair and loneliness. They also achieved their goal — a better life, first for themselves, and then for their children.

This was the overwhelming thought that possessed many immigrants. They knew how hard their own lives were and they wanted better for their children. By coming to Canada, they succeeded beyond their wildest dreams. Today the descendants of those immigrants are a vital part of this country.

While many have lost their language and customs, there are still enough who retain them to make it possible for all Canadians to have access to them. By keeping alive their traditions, Canada is made so much richer.

There are plenty of books that tell of the hard times experienced by the immigrants. This experience is not to be denied. It was a hard thing to do, and the people who did it must truly be regarded as heroes and heroines.

This book is an effort to show that there was more than just hardship in the new land. There was also joy and laughter. Nobody likes a good time and lots of fun more than someone who has a hard life.

These stories are all basically true. They happened to someone, somewhere, in one form or another. You may even recognize someone you know doing something you remember.

The title of the book refers to the fact that Vuiko Yurko was an immigrant to Canada. Thus, he became a First Generation Canadian. My father, John W Evanishen, was born in Canada, so he's second generation and I am third.

The embroidery and colors on the cover are based on a design from Halychyna, Western Ukraine, where my people came from. The design is adapted from one in the collection of my mother, Natalka Evanishen.

I am still looking for more stories or incidents similar to the ones in this collection. If anyone has a story to tell me, please write to me at this address:

Danny Evanishen
Box 1324
Summerland, BC
V0H 1Z0.

Acknowledgements

This is my first real book. I learned a lot in writing it, and I learned a lot in publishing it myself. What a lot of fun! I will do it again.

Of course, I could not do all of this myself, so I would like to thank the various people who gave me assistance of one kind or another.

For having provided the stories found in this book, I would like to thank the following people: John W and Natalka Evanishen, Johanne and Bryan Kasha, Gail Stoney, Tony Lazarowich, Olga and Bill Hamara, Helgi and Jackie Eyjolfsson, Uncle Ernie Graham, Don Woods, John VandeBerg, Uncle Barney Kuchinka, Elaine Hamm, Artie Hawrysh, Morris Diakowsky, Sonia Kindrachuk, Maureen Bendick, Linda Lazarowich, Doreen Hawrysh, Gene Kondra, George Evanishen, Dorene Fehr, Bill Luker, Clinton Weese, David Hawrysh, Steve Cheliak, Oryst Sulyma, Phil Barnard, Alex Mussick and my own fertile memory. Some of these people may not have been aware of their help, but there it is.

On the technical side, I would like to thank Dona Sturmanis and the members of the Summerland Writers & Publishers group and Carole Humphreys, who all provided aid, advice and moral support. And thanks to New Horizon Printers, who did the hard work.

Thank you also to Dorene Fehr, who did the art work and helped in so many other ways.

Photograph Credits

Thank you to the following for permission to use photographs from their collections:

Page 17   DW Evanishen
Page 26   Johanne (Evanishen) Kasha
Page 29   Natalka Evanishen
Page 41   Natalka Evanishen
Page 46   Brian Botten
Page 54   Rick Streeton
Page 63   DW Evanishen
Page 72   Fred Spooner
Page 87   DW Evanishen
Page 91   John W Evanishen
Page 96   John W Evanishen
Page 101   John W Evanishen
Page 109   Heritage Photo Co-op, Penticton,
             BC, photo by GHE Hudson
Page 119   Natalka Evanishen
Page 133   Natalka Evanishen
Back Cover photograph by Dorene Fehr

Thank you also to Ernie, Blaine and Cory Boyko and Bernie Woytiuk for their help in taking the photo of the Bullfight on Page 87.

Vuiko Yurko

Vuiko Yurko. Maybe you remember Vuiko Yurko. I never met him, but I know some people that said they did. Ukrainian guy, he was. I said was — maybe he's still alive, I don't know. Anyway, they called him Vuiko Yurko. That means Uncle George in English. I'm not sure where he lived, but from the people I talked to, he lived in a lot of places.

I had an uncle like that, who moved around a lot, but I never met him, either. My Uncle Petro came to Canada, to Manitoba, and then went to Alberta; then he went back to Ukraine, then he wound up in Saskatchewan. Maybe Vuiko Yurko was with him.

Anyhow, some people said Vuiko Yurko was a real big guy, and some said he wasn't so big. I guess to small people he looked big, and some of the things he pulled off, it seemed he had to be real big. Like I said, I never saw him, so I don't know what he looked like.

I know for sure he had a moustache, because that figures in some of the stories they told about him. And stories! They told lots of stories about Vuiko Yurko. Everybody had a story to tell about him.

The first time I heard about him was one time when I was a kid and I was in town and my uncle, my real uncle, was selling some pigs. Usually, Uncle Artie's pigs were real rowdy, because they roamed all over the place on his farm. He couldn't keep them in the pen, because they always took it apart or busted holes in it. One time, he built them a little house for the winter, and they ate the roof right off it before it even snowed once.

So I was helping my Uncle Artie with his pigs and feeling good because I was helping, like a grown-up, and the pigs were real tame this day. The guy at the stockyard asked him how come they were so easy to handle today, and my uncle said that he heard about what Vuiko Yurko used to do with his pigs, and he thought he'd try it. What happened was this:

Vuiko Yurko liked to make home brew, real good stuff. He could make that moonshine tasty and clear and strong, better than anybody. He was famous for it at one time. So one afternoon, Vuiko Yurko had his mash almost ready to cook, and he was going to cook it the next day, so he was in the barn, making sure that everything was ready. He had the still hidden out in the bush somewhere, but the mash he was keeping in the barn until it was ready. It was warmer in the barn, or something.

So Vuiko Yurko's out in the barn loading the barrel of mash onto the stone boat to take it to the still, and he hears somebody outside, and when he looks out, he sees the Mounties coming up the road on their horses.

Holy cow! What am I gonna do? He thinks real fast, and he figures that all they could find on the farm is the mash, so that's all he's got to worry about. But where to hide it? These Mounties are smart; they can find a barrel anywhere. Ah ha! There's the pig trough right by the barn, so Vuiko Yurko ups with the barrel and pours all the mash into the trough, and it's pretty full, but he figures it's dirty enough and the pigs stink pretty bad, so maybe the Mounties won't notice it.

The Mounties come into the barn with Vuiko Yurko's wife Dotsia, because she saw them riding up, and they say, "We have to look over your farm for home brew, because we know you're making it. Maybe this time we got you."

Vuiko Yurko says, "Okay, go look. I got nothing to hide from you."

And they look and they look and they poke holes in the haystacks and even in the manure pile and they look everywhere, but they don't

15

find anything. It takes them quite a while, because they want to make sure, and they look everywhere, and Vuiko Yurko goes with them everywhere, because he has other stuff they maybe shouldn't see.

Finally the Mounties are satisfied that they can't find anything and Dotsia feeds them tea in the kitchen. By now it's getting dark, and the Mounties leave and everybody goes to bed.

Next morning, Dotsia gets up early like she always does, and she goes to let out the chickens and get some eggs and then cook breakfast like she always does. Two minutes later, she comes running back into the house hollering, "Hey Yurko, come quick! All the pigs are dead!"

So he puts on his pants and goes out real fast, and sure enough, all the pigs are out in the yard lying around everywhere, except for one that's got his head in the water trough and he's drinking water to beat the band.

Vuiko Yurko goes up to one of the pigs that's lying down and pokes it, and it grunts and tries to look at him, but it can't quite focus on anything. He pokes another one, and they're all like that. Suddenly he gets a hot flash, and then he turns cold and he runs for the pigs' trough and, sure enough, it's all gone. No mash left, and the pigs all drunk as lords.

So what Vuiko Yurko did from then on when he had to handle his pigs was get them a bit tight, and then they were a whole lot easier to manage, and they really liked him for it, too.

Uncle Artie said he had so much trouble with his own pigs that he had to do something, and this idea seemed to work. He'd give them enough home brew to make them quiet, and then he could handle them. Except now nobody makes home brew any more, and liquor store booze costs too much, so now Uncle Artie has sheep and no pigs.

Pat Harach and his stone boat on his farm.

The Drunk Chicken

Vuiko Yurko was famous for his cooking at one time. He could make all kinds of meals from almost nothing and make it real tasty, too. He was especially good with chicken, because he had lots of them and he liked chickens. He knew everything about cooking them. People said it was the best they ever had when he prepared it.

It turns out that his big secret was in the way he butchered the chickens. If you kill an animal when it's excited or scared or like that, the animal's muscles all tense up and get stiff and its glands pour stuff into its system and it makes the meat tough and it doesn't taste as good as it could. Every farmer knows about that, and every hunter, too.

The problem is how to grab a chicken when it's not all excited. Have you ever seen a chicken that's not excited? Me neither. Well, Vuiko Yurko knew a few things about a few things, and he was pretty clever on top of it all, too. So he thought about it and tried to figure out when it is that he's most relaxed. It seems that he's most relaxed when he's had a couple beer or a few shots of home brew.

If he's relaxed when he's had some home brew, it's only natural that a chicken would be, too. Of course, you don't want to give the chicken too much or the meat would taste like booze, and you don't want to give it too little, or it won't work right. So Vuiko Yurko set himself to figuring out how much home brew to give the chickens, and that's where he ran into trouble.

The problem was that the chicken Vuiko Yurko picked to do his testing on was the old rooster he'd had for a few years, and this rooster was around at the time the pigs got drunk on the home brew mash. Vuiko Yurko didn't know it, but this old rooster had got in on the mash along with the pigs and got himself soused, too. Except the rooster had the sense to creep off to the hen house until he sobered up, and nobody knew anything about it.

Ever since then, the old rooster had a taste for the brew, and he had been following Vuiko Yurko around when he was making his home brew. He never took any notice of the rooster, but the rooster made sure that he got every bit of spilled mash and every stray drop of brew that got loose. That rooster was a real alcoholic.

Now, when Vuiko Yurko started his little experiment to see how much it would take to do his chickens, he didn't know that he was dealing with a bird that had so much experience. He had built up a pretty good tolerance for the booze, and every bit that Vuiko Yurko fed him made him that much worse. He got to really liking Vuiko Yurko, but he wasn't too sure how long his good luck would last.

At first, Vuiko Yurko gave the rooster just a teaspoonful of the home brew. Then he had a shot himself, and sat there and watched the rooster to see how it worked. Well, that old rooster just stood there in front of Vuiko Yurko and watched him right back. He didn't want to miss anything, either. So when nothing happened, Vuiko Yurko gave the bird two spoons, and two for himself. Again the rooster just stood there and waited for more.

After a few tries, Vuiko Yurko got a bit tight and a bit impatient. He grabbed the bird by the neck and poured a whole mickey down its throat. Plus some for himself, of course. Then he sat and watched. Well, this time it worked. Except it worked too well. That bird got so roaring drunk that when it started jumping up and down, it scared Vuiko Yurko, and he ran out of the barn into the yard.

Inside the barn, the rooster was flying around and squawking and bumping into things and trying to crow, and scaring the cattle.

Finally, it screeched into the cows' stall and they all stampeded out of the barn, breaking the door down and nearly running over Vuiko Yurko.

By the time Vuiko Yurko got the cows back and the door fixed and the dogs settled down, the rooster had passed out in the barn. And Vuiko Yurko got the idea that maybe he shouldn't be fooling around with that rooster and the home brew.

Vuiko Yurko didn't give up on his idea, though. When he had calmed down, he tried it again, but this time with a young chicken that had never had booze before. He gave her only a couple of spoons to sedate her, and she got sort of floppy and relaxed and it worked real well.

Now that nobody makes home brew any more, Vuiko Yurko uses store-bought liquor to do the job, but this costs a lot of money. So any time anybody wants to have a special chicken from Vuiko Yurko, they bring some whisky for him and he and the chickens sit down for a little party before they get down to business.

The Empty Jug

When Vuiko Yurko used to make home brew, he had a pretty good setup. He had his equipment hidden in some real secret places. He was never caught with the goods, although the Mounties used to bother him every now and then. It kind of got to be a game after a while, them trying to outsmart Vuiko Yurko or sneak up on him, but they never did catch him.

About the closest they ever came was the time he had his mash hidden in the manure pile. Somebody told the Mounties where it was, so they came over to his place all ready for the job. They didn't even pretend to look anywhere else; they went right for the pile. They were all dressed up in overalls and they had shovels and pitchforks and gloves and boots, and they knew it was going to be a dirty job. But this time they figured they had him, so they were ready to dig.

Well, those Mounties dug up that whole manure pile and spread it all over the place and they were getting so dirty and they smelled so bad. They were sweating a lot and not finding anything until finally, on the far side of the pile from where they started, they found the barrel.

They looked real happy then and worked real hard to pull the barrel out until they had it up on top of the ground, then took the top off. It was one of those barrels where the whole top comes off, not just that little hole, and they took the top off and this time they had Vuiko Yurko dead to rights.

Vuiko Yurko came closer and he said, "Gee, I don't think I ever saw that barrel before. Let me have a good look." And as he was getting close, he tripped over a pitchfork and fell on the barrel and it tipped over and all the mash ran out all over the manure pile.

"Sorry, boys, I guess I tripped."

And those poor Mounties had no evidence. Later on, somebody said that Vuiko Yurko needed to spread out his manure pile, but he knew what a dirty job it was, so he set up the whole thing himself with an anonymous telephone call to the Mounties. I don't know if that part is true, but it sure could be.

There was another time the Mounties thought they finally had Vuiko Yurko with his booze. It was winter time and the Mounties had one of those snow planes that go really fast. You remember those snow planes?

An uncle of mine, Uncle Tony, had one once. It was like a caboose that they used to hitch up behind the horse, except it had an airplane motor and propeller on the back and that made it just sail across the snow. Made a hell of a racket, though.

My father likes to tell the story of the time he was going to move his family from one school where he was teaching to another school, and he hired Uncle Tony to do it in the snow plane. So Uncle Tony did the move, and everybody was happy, except when my father went to the little store next door to say good-bye, the storekeeper told him that his neighbor was looking for him to beat him up. My father wanted to know why, and the storekeeper told him that when the neighbor heard the snow plane come roaring up, he thought it was the Mounties coming to see him, so he poured all his home brew out. He said he was going to invite my father in for a farewell drink, but now he wouldn't, even if he had some.

Anyway, this time the Mounties thought they could sneak up on Vuiko Yurko with this snow plane thing of theirs if they waited until the wind was blowing pretty hard from the north. Then if they came up fast from the south, the wind would blow the noise away from the farm and he wouldn't hear them coming.

Vuiko Yurko was in the barn checking his mash, and he didn't hear the snow plane until Dotsia, his wife, came running out of the house. "Yurko, Yurko! The Mounties are here!"

Well, Vuiko Yurko could think pretty quick. He grabbed a jug and took off right through the yard and over the fence where the snow plane couldn't go, and ran as fast as he could across the field to the bush. By the time anyone knew what was going on, he was halfway across the field. Well, what could those poor Mounties do? They really thought they had him, so they ran after him.

It was pretty hard running for the Mounties, because they had their big buffalo coats on and they were heavy, but Vuiko Yurko wasn't running too fast any more, just fast enough to keep ahead of them.

Finally, Vuiko Yurko got tired of running, and he started walking, but he was still going across the field. The Mountie finally got the snow plane out into the field and caught up to him, and the other Mounties came up and grabbed him and he looked real surprised that they were there. "What do you want, boys?"

"Give us that jug. What's in it?"

"Well, nothing. The jug is empty."

"What's this all about? What's this jug, and where are you going?"

25

Vuiko Yurko put down the jug and sat on it. "I have a sick pig and I'm going to my neighbor to get some medicine."

Well, the poor guys, they had to let him go, and they went back to the farm, but by this time Dotsia had everything hidden, and the Mounties never did find anything. Sometimes, you really had to feel sorry for them.

Tony Horbay with his snow plane.

The Outhouse

In the old days, they didn't have outhouses in the house; they were outside. I mean the toilet, you know? It was a little shack built near the house, just a hole in the ground with a little shack over it, and not too close to the house so it didn't smell too bad.

Vuiko Yurko had one of those, like everybody did. Usually, they had a pot of some kind under the bed for when it wasn't too serious, but there was a time when Vuiko Yurko wouldn't have one of those things in the house.

One night Vuiko Yurko wakes up, and he's got to go. So he goes out of the house and down the path to the outhouse, and when he's finished there, he thinks he hears a noise at the hen house, so he goes to look. Well, there's nothing there, so he goes back to bed.

Now, at this time, there was some trouble with robbers in the area. Usually, everyone knew everyone else and there was no trouble, but this time there were some bad guys that came into the neighborhood and they were stealing stuff. So Vuiko Yurko locked the door when he got back in the house, and went to bed.

He's almost asleep, and he hears somebody pounding on the door downstairs. Well, he doesn't want to get up again, so he says, "Dotsia, go see who's at the door." They were like that in those days — if he didn't want to do something, he told his wife to do it. So he tells her to go, and then he settles down to sleep again. He's tired and he doesn't want to be bothered.

Still there's somebody pounding on the door. He says again, "Wake up. There's somebody at the door." She still doesn't move, so he leans over and shakes her to wake her up. Except he's shaking empty bedcovers. She's not there!

"Now where did she get to?" he wonders. And then he gets up and puts his pants on to see who is at the door. By now he's wide awake and thinking maybe it's the police and the robbers are somewhere in the area. But where's Dotsia? So he goes to the door and opens it.

And who is at the door, all cold and mad? Well, it's his own wife! "Why did you lock me out? Where were you, why didn't you come sooner? It's cold out here," and things like that. She's pretty mad.

Well, Vuiko Yurko tries to explain that they must have missed each other when she went to the outhouse while he was checking the noise at the hen house, and they talk it over.

I guess she finally calmed down and they both went to sleep again, but in the morning she said, "Yurko, I think we need a pot under the bed." And they got one.

Typical outhouse, modeled by Jerry Evanishen.

What's That Smell?

One time, Vuiko Yurko smelled something bad in the house. He made Dotsia, his wife, clean the whole house, and he even helped, but the bad smell was still there. So he told her to clean the house again, but better this time; he had work to do in the barn.

When he got to the barn, he smelled the same bad smell. Now, barns don't always smell all that good, but you can tell when it's different. He went around the barn sniffing, but couldn't tell where it was coming from. So he went to work and cleaned up that whole big barn.

He hauled all the manure out and swept the floors and shovelled everything out and put in fresh straw, and he checked everywhere for that smell. Finally, he went to his home brew barrel and sniffed the mash. Of course, he hoped that wasn't it, but he looked anyway. Sure enough, that was it. Well, too bad, that batch went bad, so he gave it to the pigs. This time, he diluted it with water, because he didn't want the pigs to get drunk like they did last time.

But how did the smell get into the house? Must have got on his clothes or something. Oh well, the house needed two good cleanings anyway. So he dumped his mash and went to the house for lunch to tell Dotsia what the smell was.

He just got inside the house, and he could still smell the bad smell. Oh well, maybe it would take a while to get the smell out, so he opened all the doors. He didn't enjoy his lunch too much that day, so he took it outside to where there was a wind blowing, and that was better.

He went back to the barn, and that bad smell was still in there, too, so he opened all the doors. Maybe the wind would blow it away.

Everywhere he went on the farm, he could smell it — in some places stronger and in others not so strong. So he went everywhere. Maybe an animal died somewhere and he couldn't find it. He looked everywhere, but it got dark, so he had supper outside again and went to bed.

In the morning, he could still smell that bad smell, but worse, he thought. So he looked everywhere again, and that smell was everywhere and he told Dotsia she had to clean the house again, but she didn't want to. It had never been so clean. Finally she said, "Well, what does this bad thing smell like? Is it like a dead animal, or what?"

Vuiko Yurko said, "What! You mean that you haven't smelled that stink all along? How come you didn't tell me?"

And she said, "You didn't ask me. You were too busy bossing me around and you didn't ask."

Well, now he was mad, because he knew she could smell pretty good, and if she didn't smell it, then there was something funny going on. So he sat down to think about it, and she came over and looked at him, and they looked at each other and then they both started to laugh right out loud.

"Well, of course," she said. "Go wash your big, bushy moustache!"

So Vuiko Yurko went to wash out whatever it was that got caught in his moustache, and the smell was gone. He wasn't too happy about losing all that good mash, but the barn and the house needed two cleanings anyway. What he didn't like were the jokes Dotsia pulled on him after, like: "So, Yurko, how do you smell now? As bad as ever?" But she never told anyone else about it, and he sure didn't.

Vuiko Yurko's Beer

I heard some good stories about how Vuiko Yurko liked to make beer at home. He made some good beer, too, not like that stuff you buy in the liquor store. That stuff is all the same kind of taste and not very good, even. There are some smaller breweries that make good beer, but most of the real big ones only care to make money; they don't care about beer.

One of the best things about making your own beer is that it's impossible to do it the same every time, so each batch is a little bit different. You never know what you're going to get. Vuiko Yurko never made any bad beer, though.

There was one time when he thought he had made a big mistake. That was when he used molasses instead of sugar. What happened was that he was at home alone and he had the whole day put aside to make this beer. Except he didn't know that there was no sugar in the house. Dotsia had used it all for canning fruit.

Well, Vuiko Yurko didn't know what to do. He ransacked the whole house, and all he found was molasses. He looked at it and tasted it and thought, "Well, why not? It's sweet enough, and maybe it'll make a different taste."

After he had the whole batch made up and bottled, he put it away to age, like you're supposed to. Usually, it needs about three months to get really good, but sometimes you get thirsty and it doesn't last two weeks. This batch Vuiko Yurko left for the full three months.

When it came time to try this molasses beer, Vuiko Yurko fished out a bottle and opened it. It was bubbly and it looked like a nice dark beer, but it tasted awful. It was so bad that he didn't even finish the bottle. He gave it to the pigs and they drank it. They liked it just fine.

After that, Vuiko Yurko forgot all about his molasses beer. He had it stashed in the barn, and he didn't even think about it until about five years later when he was looking for some more empty bottles. He was going to pour it all out, but then he thought, "What if it's good now? Maybe it just needed to age more."

And that was the truth of the thing. He opened one bottle and took a sip, and it was beautiful, like some kind of cream ale or something. He went and got his empty bottles from somewhere else, but that molasses beer he kept for special occasions.

Sometimes his beer was pretty bubbly, too. If you put too much sugar in or something, it gets too much gas in it and it can explode. My brother made some beer like that once. You had to open it wearing welders' gloves and a face mask. Getting a beer was like going to play goalie in a hockey game.

My old friend in southern Saskatchewan, Uncle Barney Kuchinka, used to make beer. I was visiting his place one time and he said to me, "Hey, let's go out in the yard and catch a beer!"

I said, "Huh?" I mean, what can you say?

So we went outside and he gave me a big clean galvanized wash tub and he went about twenty feet away and pointed a beer bottle at me. When he opened it, the beer came shooting out and I caught some of it in the tub. What you caught you drank. That was catching a beer.

One time, Vuiko Yurko and his family were going to a picnic. He piled the car full of food and Dotsia and all the kids, and a couple of cases of beer that he had made. They drove to their neighbor's farm to see if they were going to the picnic, and both he and Dotsia went into the house to help them get ready.

While they were in the house, one of the bottles of beer popped its cap. It was so shook up by the road they had been driving on that it just built up too much pressure and blew.

The kids were sitting in the car, and they really jumped when they heard the loud Pop! when the cap flew off. They figured out pretty quick what the noise was and they thought it was pretty funny. One of them got another bottle of beer and shook it until it blew up and everybody got sprayed with beer.

Well, that was the signal for the start of a big beer war. In no time at all, there was no beer left and all the kids were soaked right through, and so was the car. There was beer and foam just about everywhere!

When Vuiko Yurko came back to the car and saw what had happened, he and Dotsia got in the car and drove right home without a word. It was one of those real quiet drives.

Vuiko Yurko left the car in the middle of the yard by the well, handed a bucket to the kids, and went into the house. He and Dotsia came out a few minutes later with some more food and some more beer. They got into the grain truck and went to the picnic alone. The kids were sure sorry that they had had so much fun with the beer.

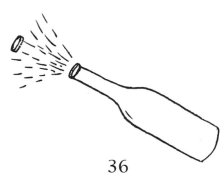

Fordelo

Vuiko Yurko never saw a car before he came to Canada. He had never even heard of such a thing. To him, a horse was the best thing for getting around, but nobody could afford them except rich people. When he had been in Canada for some time and had got himself in pretty good shape financially, he had horses. When he got his first horse, he thought he was pretty rich, too.

In Canada, lots of people had horses, and not just rich people, either. So, while he couldn't help feeling like he had finally 'arrived', he really knew that he was no better off than most other people were.

Vuiko Yurko had his horses for quite a while. He liked them better than oxen, because they could go faster and they were easier to handle. With a horse you could be friends, not like with a dumb ox. But then cars and trucks and tractors started to appear in the district.

At first, Vuiko Yurko wouldn't have anything to do with such noisy, smelly, unnatural 'masheny'. They just weren't right, and he thought they were unreliable. Well, they were, sort of, but they sure could do a pile of work when they went right.

Finally, when he saw that lots of his neighbors had cars, Vuiko Yurko thought he should get one too. He had all kinds of fun with his first car, a Model T, which he called his 'Fordelo'. Nobody taught him how to drive the thing except the dealer in town. Basically, the dealer just showed Vuiko Yurko how to get it going, and then Vuiko Yurko took off.

He drove through town tootling the little goose horn, and waved at everybody. Then he drove home to show Dotsia what he had bought. He drove into the yard and around the house and around the barn and tootled the little horn and waved at Dotsia when she came running out. She was just as excited as Vuiko Yurko was.

"Yurko, stop! Let me have a ride!"

This was the first time Vuiko Yurko had even thought about stopping. Of course, he started shouting "Whoa!" and swearing at his Fordelo and pulling on the steering wheel until it almost came off, and didn't watch where he was going, and he plowed right through the fence and into the haystack.

The car stalled in the haystack and Vuiko Yurko dug his way out with a red face. He was lucky that the haystack didn't catch on fire, like some you used to hear about.

Well, the car sat there in the haystack for a day or two until Vuiko Yurko wasn't so mad any more and he had asked around and found out how to step on all those pedals and make the car stop. He hitched up the horse and pulled the car out of the haystack and cleaned it all up.

The car dealer had given Vuiko Yurko some pointers about cranking a Model T, like, make sure you keep your thumb out and your face clear of the crank. You could tell people who hadn't followed this advice, because they had crooked thumbs and not too many teeth.

Anyhow, Vuiko Yurko got the car going again and he and Dotsia drove around and had a good time showing off to everybody in the neighborhood. They even stopped when they wanted to, after Vuiko Yurko got the hang of it.

As it turned out, Vuiko Yurko was pretty good at mechanical stuff. He had always been able to fix broken things and he could make all kinds of things, so it was natural that he would learn about cars quickly. He even got so good at this Model T that sometimes he could start it without the crank.

This was a good trick that always left people wondering. In those days, car motors started only with a crank, except for some that had stuff added after. Like, you used to be able to get an air-operated starter for a Model T.

Hardly anybody had one of those, though; everybody had to crank. And sometimes, that cranking was a pretty exciting time.

If a car was tuned up properly, it didn't take much to get it started. You just set the spark lever and the gas lever and turned the gas mixture knob, set the choke, turned on the power switch and went around the front to crank. If everything was set right, it started up on the first or second try.

If all those things weren't set up just right, though, you cranked and cranked and got red in the face and your arm got sore and sometimes the crank would kick back at you and then the kids who were always watching would cover their ears or else they'd learn some new words. For them, it was always fun.

Anyway, Vuiko Yurko figured it out that if you cranked the motor to just the right place and set everything up before you turned on the power, the spark would set off the fuel in the cylinder and the motor would turn over by itself to start. This was a great source of joy to him when it worked, and everybody would stare at him like he was magic.

The one thing that nobody could do much about was tires. In those days, the rubber wasn't very good and the roads were worse, so there were lots of flat tires. Everybody had them and everybody had a kit to fix them and everybody allowed enough time for flat tires when they went somewhere. The farther you went, the more flats you had.

Vuiko Yurko was no different. He had lots of flat tires. Where he was sometimes different, though, was when he was too tired or had too many flat tires. When that happened, he just couldn't be bothered to fix them. He just drove slower, but he kept going. It got so that his neighbor could tell when Vuiko Yurko had gone to the city, because he'd come back driving on three or four flat tires.

"Hey Vuiko Yurko! I see you're driving on your rims! How's things in the city?" he'd laugh.

Vuiko Yurko didn't think that was funny.

Dido John Hawrysh (with pipe), Baba Hawrysh, two hired men and Dido's pride and joy, his fine horses. Photo taken 1917.

Vuiko Yurko's Cars

Vuiko Yurko got to like having a car, after he got used to the idea. He always took good care of his cars, and they mostly worked well for him. That's not to say that nothing ever went wrong for him, but overall, he had good luck with them.

He used his cars to haul all kinds of stuff, not just people. Of course, he had a truck to haul the bigger stuff and the livestock, but to begin with, all he had was his Model T Fordelo, and it worked pretty hard sometimes. When cars got better and had real starters on them, he thought it was time to get one of those. It made life a lot easier when you didn't have to risk your life or your teeth with the crank.

One time after he got himself a newer car, Vuiko Yurko was visiting some friends of his and he bought a couple of young pigs from them. These were sort of wild farm pigs, but they looked real good, so he bought them. When it came time to go home, he just put them in the trunk of his car and drove away.

On the way through town, he saw someone he had to talk to, so he pulled over and they talked. One thing led to another, and pretty soon they were at the bar with a lot of neighbors and friends and they were having a real good time.

Finally, someone came in and said, "Hey! What's going on out there? There's a big crowd gathered around Vuiko Yurko's car!"

They all ran out and there were so many people you couldn't even see the car. Everybody was laughing and some of the kids were sitting on top of the car trying to poke a stick through one window that was partly open.

"Hey, you kids! What are you doing to my car?" Vuiko Yurko hollered.

The crowd let him through and he could see what the kids were doing with the stick. They were teasing the two pigs that were in the driver's seat. What happened was that the pigs didn't like being cooped up in the trunk, so they ate their way through the back seat. Now they were running around inside, making a big mess all over the car.

There was no way those excited pigs were going to let Vuiko Yurko into the car, so he told everyone to go home and then borrowed some blankets from the hotel. He covered the car up to make it dark, and finally the pigs went to sleep and he was able to get in and push them into the back seat and drive home. He said his car stank like pigs for ever after that.

Another time, he and Dotsia were driving to the next town in their car and some other guys were going in their own car. They had some kind of business there together. On the way, he stopped for gas at a filling station. As he was filling up, he saw them go by. They honked their horn and waved and he waved back.

When he was on the road again, Vuiko Yurko thought he would catch up to those other guys. He was sure his car was better than theirs and it would be no trouble, so he put his foot down and went like crazy. Showing off. Dotsia told him he was going too fast and, of course, for that he went even faster.

As he drove, he thought he should be catching up to them pretty quick, because they weren't fast drivers or anything as far as he knew. But he still couldn't see them, so he put his foot down farther. After a while, he was going down a big long hill, and he still couldn't see them, or even their dust. Well, he got mad and put his foot right down to the floor.

He made that car go as fast as it could and his dust cloud went way up into the sky. "Those guys must have seen me trying to catch them and they're trying to outrun me," he thought to himself. And away he went, faster and faster. He was sliding around the curves and gravel was flying everywhere and when he hit a bump, he flew into the air and hit his head on the roof and Dotsia was yelling at him, "What are you, crazy? You're going to kill us! Slow down!"

Sometimes he hit the roof so hard that he jammed his hat right down over his eyes, so he would take his hands off the wheel to get the hat off and he would steer with his knees, and none of this was very safe, and Dotsia was mad and scared. But he wasn't going to let those guys get away from him, so he kept driving that poor car as fast as it could go.

By some kind of blind luck, they got to town in one piece. The car was boiling over and puffing like a steam engine and there was dust all over the place. Vuiko Yurko got out of the car slowly. His knees were still a little bit weak from all that excitement. He couldn't see his friends' car, so he went into the store and asked the storekeeper where they were.

"No, we haven't seen those guys. Were they coming to town?"

Well, they weren't there. He went to the hotel and looked in the beer parlour, but they weren't there, either. He went to the restaurant and everywhere he could think of where they could be. Couldn't find them.

"Dotsia, we were supposed to meet them at the store, right? Well, where are they?"

Of course, she didn't know, so they left the car in front of the store and went into the restaurant and had a cup of coffee. They waited about a half an hour, and then they saw their friends drive up.

"Where the hell were you guys? I couldn't catch up to you nohow! How come you drove so fast, and where were you just now?" Vuiko Yurko was getting himself kind of worked up.

"What are you talking about?" they said. "The last time we saw you was when you were filling up with gas at that North Star station. We stopped at the next gas station to fill up and you went past us. We waved and honked, but you didn't hear us. You just took off like somebody had lit your tail on fire. There was so much dust that we had to wait until it cleared. Why were you in such a hurry, anyway?"

Vuiko Yurko's Model T was never as shiny as this one owned by Brian Bottensky.

Clock A Doodle Doo

Vuiko Yurko always had some chickens around the place. If you have chickens and you want more chickens, you need a rooster too, so Vuiko Yurko always had at least one rooster. He liked to keep his chickens happy.

Most of Vuiko Yurko's roosters were common, ordinary birds that did only what they were supposed to. But some were a little bit different. For example, he had one once who thought he owned not only every hen there, but also everything else on the whole farm.

This rooster would attack anything and anybody he thought was threatening the hens, and he even used to attack the tractor if it got too close to his ladies. This bird wasn't any too bright. One day, Vuiko Yurko found him dead by the side of the road. He must have tried to attack a car, but they move a lot faster than a tractor, so he lost that battle.

Then Vuiko Yurko got another couple of roosters when they were just young chicks. The guy he got them from had to get rid of both of them, and Vuiko Yurko was soft-hearted enough to think they would get along if they grew up together. He took them home and put them in with the chickens.

Everything went along fine for a while, but then, as they got older, the smaller rooster seemed to be losing out. The bigger one had all the hens and the little guy had only what he could sneak when the big guy wasn't watching.

Vuiko Yurko felt sorry for the little guy and tried to give him to somebody who needed a rooster, but everybody had one. He was still trying to figure out what to do about it when the smaller rooster disappeared. Vuiko Yurko figured maybe a fox got him or something.

A few days later, Vuiko Yurko's neighbor came into his yard.

"Hey Vuiko Yurko, you remember that red rooster you were trying to get rid of a while ago? You still got him?"

"Gee, no, he disappeared a few days ago."

"Well, I got him now, I think. He came over to my place the other day and chased my old rooster away. He's taking real good care of those hens, so I guess I'll keep him."

Another time when Vuiko Yurko needed a rooster, he got one from a friend of his. The friend was getting rid of all his chickens, but this rooster was a real character, so he didn't particularly want to kill him.

"This is a real special rooster," said the neighbor. "He's survived three raccoon attacks and two dog attacks. He's a tough old bird, so I figure he deserves to live. The last time he got grabbed by a raccoon was pretty strange. I heard a commotion out in the yard one evening, so I grabbed my rifle and ran out.

"I got outside just in time to see this raccoon running up that big tree in my front yard. Well, I just hauled off and shot into the branches and leaves where I figured he'd be. Maybe scare him away or something. I didn't expect to hit him, but I guess I did, because he fell out of the tree dead. And right on top of him fell this rooster, alive and squawking. I didn't even know the coon had him."

"Well, this must be one tough old bird," said Vuiko Yurko. "I guess I can start an Old Folks' Home for Roosters."

What the friend didn't tell Vuiko Yurko was that the rooster had failed crowing school. He had missed the last lesson, so he went more like "Cock a doodle...!" instead of the usual "Cock a doodle doo!" He always missed that last note.

That last note wasn't a problem; it was even kind of cute. The problem was that somewhere along the line, this rooster's clock had got busted. He crowed at every hour of the day or night. Even locked up in the hen house at night, he was always braying away with his half-finished "Cock a doodle...!"

It took some time to get used to the constant crowing, but Vuiko Yurko felt some kind of real affection for this bird, so he got used to it. He would point out the rooster to all his visitors and tell them the story of all his miraculous escapes. You could tell he was real proud of his rooster.

One night, Vuiko Yurko was lying in bed half asleep. He was just lying there in a kind of stupor, sort of thinking, and he thought he'd like to know what time it was. He had one of those bonging clocks that strikes on the hour, and when he heard the clock striking, he started to count the bongs.

He counted and counted, nearly asleep, and when he reached twenty-two, he suddenly sat bolt upright. "What's going on here? That's my good expensive clock! What's wrong with it?"

He was just about to get up when he heard the noise again, and it wasn't the clock after all. It was his wonderful rooster crowing and crowing, and not the clock at all!

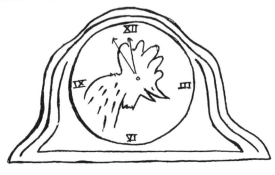

Driving Cars

Vuiko Yurko was a pretty good driver. By that, I mean he wasn't ever involved in a serious accident. Oh sure, he did a little bit of fender-bending, but who didn't? And he did get stopped by the police a few times, but that was mostly for speeding. Not real serious.

He was pretty good at finding his way, too. He hardly ever got lost, and then only if he was given wrong directions. He could read English okay, so he was able to keep an eye on the road signs, too. He wasn't too sure about those new-fangled signs the highways department put up a few years ago, though.

You know the signs I mean. They have pictures on them instead of words. Like, a little bed with a person in it is supposed to mean there's a place to stay ahead. Some of those signs are real big if the town you're coming to has lots of stuff in it, like gas, repairs, food, hospital, information and lodging.

"I spend my whole life learning English," said Vuiko Yurko, "and then they take it away and give me pictures. I could always read pictures. Now what do I need English for?" Chinese writing, he used to call those signs.

He thought the sign with only one big question mark on it was funny. It's supposed to mean that there's a tourist information center ahead, but Vuiko Yurko always said, "Look! They got something in that town and they don't even know what it is!"

Vuiko Yurko usually kept up with new developments in cars. When they came out with seat belts, he was one of the first to get them. He always used them. Always. "Keeps me in the car on those rough roads," he used to say. Some of those roads were pretty rough, and sometimes he didn't drive as slow as he maybe should.

One time, his car wasn't working and he borrowed a car from a friend of his, and this car didn't have seat belts. When he got to the meeting in town, everybody was waiting outside because he had the key to the hall. He parked the car, undid the belt and got out of the car.

Of course, as soon as he stood up to get out of the car, his pants fell down. He forgot he wasn't in his own car and just undid his own belt in his pants instead of the seat belt. That got the meeting off to a good start, anyway.

After a while there was a law passed that said you must wear seat belts in the car. Well, when that happened, Vuiko Yurko all of a sudden wasn't so excited about wearing his seat belts any more. He thought the government was interfering in his life too much. So sometimes he just forgot to do them up.

One time he was going somewhere and he was listening to the radio and the news was telling him something about the government that he didn't like. He got mad and undid his seat belt. He would show them that they couldn't push him around.

Just then, he saw a Mountie car ahead of him with its lights flashing. Oh oh. Road block. He stopped his car and the Mountie finished up with the car ahead and came back to Vuiko Yurko. That gave him time to do up his seat belt again. It was one of that kind that come over your shoulder, and Vuiko Yurko was kind of nervous, so he kind of fumbled around with it a bit, trying to do it up so they wouldn't see.

The Mountie came to Vuiko Yurko's car and put his head in the window and said, "Good morning, sir. I see your seat belt is done up. Have you had it done up all the time?"

"Oh yes, I always do it up as soon as I get in the car at home."

"Well then, you must be a pretty good driver. You have your seat belt hooked up right through the steering wheel!"

Well, Vuiko Yurko turned bright red and the Mountie was laughing so hard that he didn't even give Vuiko Yurko a ticket. Sometimes you had to be a little bit lucky.

Vuiko Yurko had lots of cars like this 1937 Ford owned by Rick Streetonchuck.

The Moose Ride

There were always lots of wild animals running around in the bush near Vuiko Yurko's farm. Of course, there were more in the old days before there were so many people around. Now you don't see many animals.

When Vuiko Yurko first came to Canada, he went to a homestead where there was lots of bush. He looked at some land in the south, on the prairies, but there were no trees there. To him, trees and wood were something very special.

In the old country, all the forest land was owned by the big rich landowners, and they charged the poor peasants an arm and a leg for the wood. If you sneaked into the woods and cut down a tree, the landlord could have you put to death for that. It was pretty bad over there.

So trees were important to most of the pioneers. That's why not many of Vuiko Yurko's people settled in the south where the land may have been good and it didn't need much work to be cleared. They went to where there were trees.

At first, all that the pioneers owned was what they had brought with them. Sometimes, it wasn't very much at all. The guys that sold them their passage were telling them all kinds of lies about how the government would give them whatever they needed to run a farm. Some people sold everything in the old country and came with nothing.

Vuiko Yurko was a little better prepared. He wasn't going to leave behind all those good tools that he had collected or made himself. He knew you couldn't replace some of his tools, and he didn't believe everything he was told, either.

When he got to the homestead, Vuiko Yurko looked around and was extremely pleased with all the trees that were his. He felt really lucky. Later on, he found out how much work it took to clear the land for growing stuff, but right now he was happy.

The first thing he had to do was make some kind of a house to live in. He wanted to have things ready for the rest of his family when they arrived. He dug a hole in the side of a little hill and made his first home there. He cut some trees and put up a sort of roof inside the hole, so that it wouldn't collapse on him, and hung up a blanket for a door. Then he set to work clearing his land for planting.

Vuiko Yurko was lucky he was able to buy a small rifle. He used it to hunt for his food. Until his garden was ready, there wasn't much other kind of food to be had. He got mostly small animals, like rabbits and grouse and such, but sometimes he was lucky and got a deer close enough to home that he didn't have to carry the meat a long way.

One time, he was coming back from working on the land, and he heard some kind of commotion going on at his house. He went up quietly and saw that a moose had stuck its head in the doorway of his house and got its antlers caught on the blanket he used for a door.

Vuiko Yurko looked at the moose. He was never going to get a moose any closer than this to his house. The problem was, the rifle was in the house, and the moose was filling up the doorway. Right about there, Vuiko Yurko quit thinking logically. He just acted.

He got his big knife out of his pocket, opened it up and stuck it between his teeth. He jumped onto the back of that moose and tried to cut its throat before it knew what was happening. Well, it didn't work that way. The moose jerked its head back and knocked the knife out of Vuiko Yurko's mouth and gave him a bloody nose. He was lucky the knife didn't get shoved down his throat.

The moose ripped the blanket off the house when it jerked its head back and then it took off running. Later on, Vuiko Yurko said he should have jumped off right there, but his head was still ringing from the bump on the nose, and he just hung on.

The moose tried to buck him off and then just ran off through the bushes. Those moose can run awful fast when they're scared, and they don't have any problem pushing bushes aside. Vuiko Yurko was hanging on for all he was worth, but the branches were scratching him up pretty bad and his clothes were getting ripped.

Finally, his head cleared a bit, and the next time they ran by a big tree, Vuiko Yurko made one big effort and jumped off the moose, grabbing its antlers on the way. He twisted its head around so that it ran smack into the tree and broke its neck. Vuiko Yurko managed to miss the tree and rolled to a stop a little way off. Everything was suddenly real quiet.

Vuiko Yurko lay on the ground and caught his breath. He took stock of himself and found that he wasn't injured, just scratched a lot and sort of messed-up. But now he had a good supply of meat. All he had to do was carry it all back to his house, wherever that was.

Oxen

Vuiko Yurko had some oxen. In those early days everyone had oxen. Remember oxen? They were like great big cows, but not as easy to get along with. That was in the days before everybody had horses, and long before there was much machinery of any kind.

In the old country, hardly anybody had horses. The big rich landowners had them, of course, because they had a lot of money and they liked to show off. In the fields, though, the peasants worked mostly with oxen.

In Canada the first settlers wanted oxen, because they understood them. They didn't have much experience with horses and they couldn't afford them and they thought horses were beyond their station in life anyway.

So Vuiko Yurko had some oxen. He had two that were evenly matched and they worked well together. Not like some teams where one worked and the other just sort of dragged along. They were good oxen. But for all that, they were still oxen, with minds of their own sometimes.

Normally, a well-trained ox will do what it's trained to do, but sometimes it just does whatever it wants to. For example, when it's hot and there are lots of flies and the oxen have been pulling the plow all day, you never drive them where they can see or smell water. Sure as hell, they'll go straight for the slough to get in and cool off, and all you can do is pull the plow up so you don't get a furrow dug to the slough.

One morning, Vuiko Yurko got his oxen hooked up to the stone boat so that he could go and pick some of his nice crop of rocks from the field. He drove the team to the front of the house and went in to get his lunch. He talked to Dotsia for a while and by the time he came out of the house, one ox was on the ground fast asleep.

"Come on, you lazy brute," he yelled at the ox. "You slept all night and now when I want to go to work you have to sleep all day, too?"

He poked at the ox and bopped it on the head with his lunch pail, but all the ox did was open one eye and then go back to sleep. No way he was going to get up. Well, what can you do? The only way to move that ox was with blasting powder, but Vuiko Yurko wasn't quite ready for that. He had other things in the yard to keep him busy. Always lots to do on a farm.

He went to the barn and did the work he had to do there and came out again, but the ox was still sleeping. Then he went to the garden and did some work there, and looked again. No luck. By now, it was getting to be time for lunch, so he went to the house and opened his lunch pail and sat down with Dotsia and ate his lunch.

He finished that and the ox was still down, so he lay down for a nap. Later, Dotsia shook him awake and said, "Quick, the ox just got up."

"Okay, Dotsia, make me another lunch! I'll work right through supper."

While Dotsia made him a lunch, he hurried out. Of course, by the time he got there, the other ox was just settling down for a nap. Vuiko Yurko didn't get much done in the field that day.

Another time, Vuiko Yurko had an interesting experience with his animals. One of his oxen had just died and he had to go to town that day with a load of something, so he thought he would hook up the ox with one of his cows to the wagon. A cow is a lot like an ox, and one of his cows was a real big one and pretty tame, so why not try it?

He hooked them both up to the wagon and then drove them around the yard to see how it would work. Seemed to be okay, so he filled the wagon and off they went. They went pretty slow and everything was fine. It took longer, but they got to town and Vuiko Yurko got rid of his load and everybody had a good laugh at Vuiko Yurko's funny-looking team.

"Don't laugh, boys!" he said. "If it works, don't laugh at it."

He did his shopping in town and then drove the team home again. Everybody who saw them had to laugh, but Vuiko Yurko was good-natured about it. The ox had been to town lots of times and knew its way home, so Vuiko Yurko thought he'd have a nap in the wagon as they went along. He had done this lots of times, too.

When he finally woke up, it was dark. We must be home by now, he thought. But there was no sign of anything. It was pitch black and he couldn't see at all. He had no idea where he was, so he thought he'd better spend the night right where he was and go home in the morning.

He unhooked the ox and the cow and hobbled them, made himself some supper, and curled up for the night. When he woke up in the morning, he stood up and looked around. There was the wagon and there was the ox and there was the cow. But where was he?

He climbed a little hill that was nearby and looked down into town. He was only over the hill from town! They hadn't gone hardly anywhere! He looked down at the wagon and saw a big round circle made by the wagon wheels and the animals with their hooves.

He stared at this big circle and made his brain wake up, and finally he figured out what had happened. The cow had got tired because it wasn't used to working so hard, and the ox was strong enough that it just pushed toward the cow. Without Vuiko Yurko to correct them, they had walked in a big circle for hours and hours while Vuiko Yurko was napping.

Eventually they got home and Dotsia wanted to know where they had been all night.

"Oh, I stayed in town too long and slept along the road," Vuiko Yurko said.

The people in town never did figure out what that big circle was just over the hill, either.

Artie Hawrysh and his snow plow.

The Snow Plow Club

Vuiko Yurko lived on a farm that was a few miles from town. He used to go to town quite often in the summer, driving his horses or his car. Getting to town was always a problem in winter, though, because of all the snow.

In those days, the highways department wasn't very big and they didn't have a lot of money to do any extra work, like plowing the roads to everybody's farm. They would do the main roads and that was about it. Of course, if you lived on a road where there was a highways man or a government man living, it was no problem. They did those roads all the time.

Mostly, though, the farmers were left to their own devices. They got in and out as best they could or they stayed home. Vuiko Yurko thought about this for a few years. He had lots of time to think, being snowed in all the time. He finally figured it out and talked to some of his neighbors to see about forming a co-operative snow plow club.

This idea of such a club was fairly common, I hear. Farm people could be pretty good at forming co-operative organizations like that to get things done, and Vuiko Yurko was pretty good at getting things organized.

My Uncle Artie was a member of such a club one time. He said they had a lot of fun and sang a lot of songs and drank some wine, too. They had one winter without much snow, so they spent their time at their club meetings writing a song. If you ever heard the song called 'Viter Duye' or 'Viter Viye', that's where it came from. If you have heard it, you'll also know what kind of meetings they had.

Anyhow, a bunch of Vuiko Yurko's neighbors got together at his place one time and formed a club. They wrote to the highways department and told them what they wanted to do, and the highways department made a deal with them. If those guys would keep their roads and some others clear, too, the department would throw in some money and maybe an old plow if they could find one.

Well, everybody was thrilled when this letter from the department arrived. They had a big meeting and broke out some wine and had a great big party, singing songs and telling stories.

They got everything ready that summer. They had lots of meetings. They got an old plow from somewhere and fixed it up and stored it at somebody's farm and made up a schedule of who was supposed to work on it and when. They opened a bank account and the highways department sent them some money to put in it. They were ready.

That next winter, there was practically no snow. Maybe just a little bit here and there. It was so bad that everybody was worried about their crops not getting enough moisture next growing season. It hardly snowed at all, and all the snow plow club meetings were taken up with rewriting the work schedule and drinking wine and singing songs. Even if there was no real work to do, it was still a fun time.

The next winter, they were all ready again. They had meetings every couple of weeks, because they heard that it was supposed to really snow that winter, and because the meetings were fun. They were going to be just as ready as they were last winter. So far, they hadn't had the plow out even once, except when they first got it.

One night, it snowed. It snowed and snowed. In the morning, you couldn't even see from the house to the barn. Of course, everybody wanted to get out and get the plow working, but there was just no way. You couldn't even get out of the house, let alone the yard.

They had to wait until the snow packed itself down a bit so they could get around. It sure wasn't going to melt for a while. It was cold. Finally, some of the guys got out with their sleighs and went to find the snow plow. At first, they couldn't remember where it was. Nobody had seen it for over a year.

Then somebody remembered whose farm it was at. "Oh yeah, Nykola, but he's away for a couple of months. Let's go to his farm and get it."

So they all went out to the farm and went to where they had last seen the plow. They dug into a huge snow drift and worked at it for an hour, but there was no plow there. Nykola had obviously moved it. Oh, there was some swearing then, and they decided to have a meeting.

"Where is that Nykola? Let's phone him and ask him where he put it."

No, they couldn't do that. He had gone away to the city to look for work, and nobody knew just where he was. They went back to his farm with long poles and shovels and started going all over, poking holes in the snowdrifts, trying to find the plow.

They spent a few hours poking and they found all sorts of machinery, but no plow. Finally they gave up and had a meeting. That sort of settled everybody down. Wine will do that.

By the time Nykola came back, the snow was almost all gone. He went to Vuiko Yurko's farm to see how the snow plow club was doing.

"Where's the plow?" hollered Vuiko Yurko. "We went to your place, but we couldn't find it."

"I don't have it," said Nykola. "I was going away, so I took it to Fred's place. Ask him."

Well, Fred had gone away, too. He went to visit his brother down East and must have forgotten all about the plow. They had another meeting and sang some more songs and made up another work schedule and then went over to Fred's place to get the plow.

Nobody was home at Fred's, so they searched all over the farm, but they couldn't find the plow. Finally, somebody suggested they telephone Fred and ask him. Good idea. They had another meeting and telephoned Fred and he told them where he had left the plow.

"Oh yeah," Fred said. "I guess I forgot about it." He told them it was in his machine shed. Nobody had thought to look there.

They all went over to Fred's again and found the plow. They pulled it out and hauled it to Vuiko Yurko's barn and cleaned it up and oiled it and had another meeting right there in the barn. Now they were ready. Let it snow!

But it didn't. That was all they had that winter. At least the plow was ready for next year, and they had had some good meetings.

Tommy Douglas

Vuiko Yurko didn't have a whole lot to do with politics at first. The early pioneers didn't have any time for that kind of thing; they were too busy trying to survive. And, in the old country, they had been mostly peasants who had no political ideas at all. Lots of them couldn't even read, because the big landowners thought it would be easier to control them if they didn't know anything.

Vuiko Yurko was just like everybody else. He was scratching out a bare living from the land and going off to work wherever he could to make some money to buy food and things. After a while, the immigrants began to learn more English and started to take more of an interest in this country that had let them in.

In those early days, when an immigrant had a vote, he usually used it to help the party that he thought had helped him. Of course, a lot of votes were bought with whisky and kobasa, but that's the way it goes when you don't understand what's going on. New country, new customs, new language, and all that.

Later on, when people were getting a little bit more comfortable and knowledgeable and were finding out that their vote could really make a difference, they jumped in with both feet. They had a lot of fun and made a lot of noise and even got some good things done.

One of the best people ever in government was Tommy Douglas. Everybody respected him because he was such a good person. Even the other political parties listened to him. Vuiko Yurko heard about him, and he and a bunch of his friends went to hear him speak.

The meeting was in town, with Tommy speaking for the CCF party and another guy for the Liberal party. When everybody got to the hall, there were so many people that the meeting organizers thought they'd better have the meeting out in the yard.

It was summer and a nice day, so everybody went outside. They weren't ready with any kind of a speakers' platform, so they just threw some boards on top of an old manure spreader and the speakers climbed up on it to speak.

Tommy Douglas was the first speaker. He looked around at the people and then he looked down at his feet and said, "You know, this is the first time I ever spoke on a Liberal platform."

Well, the place went crazy. Everybody thought that was pretty funny, except the Liberal guy. He didn't think it was funny at all. He looked down at Tommy, because Tommy was a real small person, and he said, "I eat little guys like you for breakfast."

Tommy, real quick, said: "That would be the first time you had more brains in your stomach than your head." He was a bright one, Tommy was, and funny.

When I was a kid, I was at a teachers' convention with my mom and dad and Tommy Douglas was the main speaker. I still remember a story he told that day. It was about a Canadian soldier who was posted to France during the war.

This soldier was on guard duty one morning, and a wedding party went by. It was a real big affair, and the soldier asked a guy who was walking by, "Who got married?"

The French man said, "Je ne sais pas." That's French for 'I don't know.'

Later that afternoon, a funeral went by and the soldier asked the same guy who happened to be going by again, "Who died?"

The French man said again, "Je ne sais pas."

The soldier said, "Well, he certainly didn't last very long, did he?"

Tommy Douglas

The Bullfight

Vuiko Yurko got the idea for a bullfight. It's hard to say where this idea came from; maybe he read about it in a book or a newspaper. Now, Vuiko Yurko wasn't cruel or anything like that. He probably didn't know that in most places they kill the bulls at the end, and he sure didn't know about the picadors and such guys who stab the bulls with spears to make them mad. It makes them mad, all right, but it also hurts them. It's not very nice.

So Vuiko Yurko was going to have a bullfight. It's a good thing he's got a patient wife. Dotsia had been through a lot of his schemes, and she always survived intact. Not that he was always doing something harebrained; usually his ideas were a lot of fun and sometimes even profitable. But there was always something about them that was at least a little bit unusual.

Something like a bullfight was already unusual all by itself, and it sure was going to be fun. So the first thing Vuiko Yurko needed was a bull. Well, he didn't have one of them. The nearest he had was one old steer that had a real mean streak in him.

The problem with the steer was that because it was so ornery, Vuiko Yurko had cut off its horns. They weren't very long to begin with, but he was starting to do some damage to the other animals. As it was now, he was still butting them, but at least he wasn't poking holes in them like before.

The bull question settled, Vuiko Yurko now set about making a pair of horns for the beast. He had found some old moose antlers in the bush a long time ago, but had just left them where they were. Now he needed them, so he went and got them. But how to fix them onto the steer?

He drove the steer into one of those pens that hold the cows tight so that the vet can do whatever he needs to, and he tied the steer's head up to the pen. To fix the antlers on, he used an old car tire tube cut up, and just tied them on real tight. When he let the steer go, it looked like it had got its head caught in a tree and had a toothache to boot.

There was no way that animal was going to wear those antlers. It bucked and swung around all over the place, and it finally threw them off. Antlers are tough, though, and so is Vuiko Yurko.

He picked them up and dusted them off and next day put them on again. This time he had a bit of a treat to feed the steer, and it wasn't so bad.

After a few weeks, he had the steer wearing the antlers longer and longer, and finally it seemed to kind of like having them on. It always got a treat when the antlers appeared, and they didn't hurt, although they felt funny. Even made the steer look kind of fiercer. To tell the truth, the antlers made the steer look kind of stupid, but you couldn't tell that to the steer. Or to Vuiko Yurko, either.

Okay, that was settled. Next thing was where to have this bullfight. Well, no problem. The corral was pretty big, and the steer wouldn't get away once he was in there.

Now, what about a cape? You've got to have some kind of a red cape to wave around in front of the bull, so that he can chase it. That's what it's all about, after all. You go in waving this red thing at the bull, and he gets mad and starts charging at it, and you prove how much of a hero you are by standing there trying not to get killed. Sounds pretty smart, right?

So Vuiko Yurko got hold of some of Dotsia's curtains from the house and there was the cape. The curtains were more of a wine color, but it was close enough. Of course, Dotsia was shaking her head the whole time he was doing all this, but he was having fun, so let him go and do it.

When the big day arrived and the neighbors all came over to see this thing happen, there was Vuiko Yurko with his big wine-red cape, and there was the steer with the antlers rubber-banded onto its head. That was about all the preparation he made. He wasn't going to wear any of those funny clothes he saw in the pictures. Can you imagine Vuiko Yurko wearing tights and a hat that looks like a mouse's ears?

Vuiko Yurko herded the steer into the corral with the help of some of the audience. The kids were really excited about the whole thing, and the men were mostly amused; the women thought it was all pretty silly.

Finally, the steer was in the corral and Vuiko Yurko jumped over the fence and waved his red cape at the steer. The steer just stood there with the antlers stuck on his head. He was waiting for his treat. Well, the whole thing looked like it was grinding to a halt until one of the boys pulled out his slingshot and fired a rock at the steer's backside.

You could hear the Thwack! as the rock hit the steer, and the sting went right through its thick hide. In a second, it was bucking all over the corral and bouncing off the fence and everybody had to jump off the fence and run. Then the steer spotted Vuiko Yurko standing there, and took a big run at him.

There was dust and snorting and pounding hooves and people yelling all over the place. And there was Vuiko Yurko standing there, waiting for the steer. The steer charged him and Vuiko Yurko jumped out of the way all right, but his fancy red cape got caught on the steer's antlers.

Now we had a mad steer with moose antlers on its head, in a full gallop, with a curtain over its head so it couldn't see anything. That dumb steer never slowed down one little bit. It just kept charging and slammed through the corral like a freight train. It busted the fence all up and just kept on going.

Vuiko Yurko picked himself up off the ground and dusted himself off, and then just kind of stood there and looked at his broken-up corral. He hadn't expected things to turn out quite like they did.

Later on, they found the steer out in the field without the antlers and the cape. The steer seemed to have forgotten all about the whole thing, but Vuiko Yurko and his neighbors sure didn't. To begin with, they had to repair the corral and go find Dotsia's curtains.

Chickens in the Classroom

Chickens. What can you say about chickens? Well, you can say lots of things about chickens. Only, if you don't have anything good to say, don't say much around Vuiko Yurko. He likes chickens. He always had some and he always took good care of them.

It's not like Vuiko Yurko fed the chickens and cleaned out their hen house or anything; his kids did that. But he always made sure it was done and that his birds were happy. They always had at least one rooster around, and the kids did a good job feeding and cleaning and gathering eggs, so they were doing okay.

One day, Vuiko Yurko had to go into town to pick up Dotsia, his wife. She had spent a couple of days in town with her sister, and they were going to do some shopping and stay overnight and come home the next afternoon.

The kids were old enough to be left home alone, so Vuiko Yurko wasn't worried about anything.

"Don't forget the chickens," was all he said.

Well, the kids weren't about to forget the chickens. They knew how much their father thought of them. So away went Vuiko Yurko. The kids just carried on like they normally would. The only thing is, they were hoping that nothing happened to the chickens, because then they would really hear it.

Since it was winter, there wasn't a whole lot of food running around loose for the foxes and coyotes to eat, and the kids knew that. When they locked up the hen house at night they went all around it twice and made sure that there were no holes in it.

Next morning when they got up, they went to let the chickens out. On the way to the hen house, Sonia saw a great big skunk scuttling away under the barn.

"Oh oh," she said. "Look at that skunk! Right in broad daylight, too!"

They ran over to the hen house and saw tracks in the snow all around it. Skunk, coyote, and maybe a weasel, they thought.

"Well, what are we going to do now?" said Sonia. "We have to let the chickens out to eat and drink, but we have to go to school, too. I wish we still had a dog. Then we wouldn't have to worry."

"How come we never worried about it before?" asked Metro.

"There was always someone home before," said Sonia. "So what are we going to do?"

They thought and thought, and then finally decided they would take the chickens to school with them. It wasn't too far, and the chickens were pretty tame, so they thought they could handle them okay. They'd just have to leave for school a little earlier than usual, that's all.

They let the chickens out of the hen house and fed them a little bit and carried water and dumped the ice out of the water dish, then went into the house and had their breakfast. Somebody always kept looking out the window, though, to be sure.

When they were done breakfast, they filled up the stove with wood and got ready for school. Then they went outside and told the chickens what was in store for them.

"Okay, you chickens! We're worried you'll get eaten by wild animals, so we're taking you to school with us. You're too fat anyway, and the exercise will do you good."

They started herding the chickens down the path across the field, and Metro filled his pockets with grain. He held some in his hand and walked backwards, with the chickens running after him trying to get at the grain. The trip took quite a lot longer than usual, and by the time they all got to school, everyone was inside.

As soon as they got there, Sonia ran in to tell the teacher what they had done and why they were late. Of course, as soon as the other kids heard the news, they all rushed to the window to see the chickens. What an uproar!

The teacher was a good person, though. He didn't see anything wrong with what Vuiko Yurko's kids had done, and since it was Friday anyway, he decided that having the chickens around would be okay. Metro scattered some grain on the ground and Sonia found a bowl for their water. With the snow fence up around the schoolyard, they figured the chickens wouldn't go too far and they could easily keep an eye on them through the window.

All morning, Sonia kept getting up and looking out the window. She saw that the chickens mostly huddled together, trying to keep warm. The temperature had been dropping ever since early morning, and it looked like they were in for a real cold spell. The poor chickens were sure getting cold. Even though they can fluff out their feathers, too much cold can kill a chicken.

At recess, the kids all ran outside and played with the chickens and fed them and got them fresh water. Before noon, though, it was getting awful cold and the wind was starting to blow the snow around in the schoolyard.

"Sonia," said the teacher, "I used to live on a farm, and I know that if we don't do something, those chickens of yours will freeze to death out there. Why don't you bring them in? We'll do a lesson on chickens today."

Well, this was a great idea! In no time at all, the chickens were running around the classroom and everybody was having a good time. Of course, there was a certain amount of a mess on the floor, but all the kids agreed to pitch in and clean up at the end of the day.

Finally, the teacher told everybody that they should go home early, since the weather was going to get worse, so they put the chickens outside and everybody pitched in and cleaned up. Just as they were finishing, they could hear the jingling of a sleigh. They went to the window and saw Vuiko Yurko out in the yard, staring at all the chickens.

When everything was finally explained, Vuiko Yurko had a good laugh along with everyone else. They all piled into the sleigh with the chickens and rode home. So the chickens got a sleigh ride out of the day, too. After that, Vuiko Yurko always claimed that he had the best-educated chickens in the whole country because they had been to school.

The Fair Judge

Back in the old days, there wasn't much for law and court cases in the rural areas. This was because there weren't many people there, and there just weren't enough police and judges to take care of everybody. Mostly, this wasn't a problem, because most people were too busy trying to scratch out a living to do bad things.

There were some people who didn't mind helping themselves to someone else's things, but there weren't many like that, and usually they were forced out of the district by the rest of the people. The usual way to do things was, if you really needed something, you asked for it. If there was nobody to ask, you took whatever it was you needed so badly and then replaced it later or paid for it.

There were always little disputes, but nothing like now. These days, people have so little to do that they have lots of spare time to think up all kinds of mischief. Back then, though, there just wasn't any idle time at all.

Usually when there was a dispute of some kind in the district, people would come to Vuiko Yurko. It didn't take long before everybody recognized that he was a pretty sharp guy. Like Solomon, they said; he could see right to the heart of the dispute and come up with a solution that was as fair and as sensible as the people involved. Even those who had things decided against them had to admit when they cooled off that Vuiko Yurko was usually right.

There came a time, though, when the authorities, the government or somebody, started to take notice of the increasing population of the district. Probably some politician who thought he could get some votes if he made a big fuss. So a policeman was stationed in the district. He lived in the village and either walked or hitched a ride to anywhere he had to go. Later he had a horse, but at first, there wasn't even money for that.

The policeman was one of the Royal Canadian Mounted Police (or North West Mounted Police, in those days) that took care of the law where there were no cities with their own police. That meant most of the country, so the police were scattered pretty thinly. This one policeman was supposed to take care of everything in a huge area. He did the best he could, but he wasn't always able to get to the scene of any trouble right away, so things were still often handled by the people involved, with the help of their neighbors.

When there got to be more people, the troubles began to get bigger. When you get lots of people together in one place, there's a pretty good chance that at least a few will not be the cream of the earth.

And so it went. Just the presence of the Mountie kept things at a reasonable level. If matters got out of hand, you could threaten to go for the Mountie, or if the thing was serious enough, you actually went and got him.

The cases where the Mountie was involved were usually more serious, and if you had done something wrong, you could expect harsher treatment from the law than from your neighbors. Often, if you had done something really serious, the Mountie would take you to his office, and lock you up there until he could get you to the city where there was a judge.

This whole system took a lot of time for justice to be done, and it wasn't always justice, because it was all so far away from where the disputes or crimes happened. City judges didn't always know what it was like in the rural areas.

So judges started to come out to the country. Circuit judges, they were called. They would travel to all the outlying communities once a month or so to handle all the cases that had built up. The judge would arrive and all the people who were charged with something or who had grievances would come there and they would have a court.

These courts were something of a social event. At certain times of the year there isn't too much to do on the farm, and people would go to court, just to see what was going on. This was fine with the judges, because then everybody knew that the law was in control now.

The judge in Vuiko Yurko's district was a success right from the start. He was a smart one, and before he even went out to the district, he had the Mountie find out for him who was the most respected man in the district. This turned out to be Vuiko Yurko, and here's what they did:

The night before the court was going to be held, the judge and the Mountie and Vuiko Yurko would all sit down together in the Mountie's house to discuss the cases over a bottle of home brew or whisky. They went over everything together, and the Mountie knew the facts and the judge knew the law and Vuiko Yurko knew the people.

The Mountie would say, "Here's what Peter did, and everyone knows it."

"Oh yeah," Vuiko Yurko would say, "Peter did that, all right, but he knows it was wrong and he's sorry for it. He's really a good man, and he's got a bunch of kids, so don't be too hard or they'll suffer more than he will."

"Okay," the judge would say, "but we still have to give him some kind of penalty so he'll remember it, and so other people won't do it."

And they would arrive at all kinds of solutions, and next day in court, the judge would make all these decisions and impose all these fines and so forth, and everybody was so surprised and impressed and pleased with how fair and how smart that judge was.

"You know," they would say, "that judge is almost as smart as Vuiko Yurko!"

Bernie Woytiuk and Blaine Boyko tried to have a bullfight like Vuiko Yurko's. It didn't work.

The Falcon

When Vuiko Yurko lived on the farm, he always had chickens and roosters. He had always liked them, ever since he was a little boy. Of course, in the old country, they meant a lot to any family lucky enough to have any. Sometimes, all they had to eat were the eggs and the chickens themselves.

So Vuiko Yurko always had chickens and roosters around. Some were kind of special, and Vuiko Yurko could always spot the ones that had something extra about them. Like that old rooster that got into the home brew mash with the pigs and got himself drunk. Vuiko Yurko had a soft spot for that rooster.

He had another special rooster that was with him for years. When it was just a young chick, it somehow got into the habit of following Vuiko Yurko around. Everywhere he went, there was the rooster. When it got a little bit older, it would even go to town with him. When he drove away, the rooster was sure to jump up on the wagon and go with him.

Vuiko Yurko knew right away that he could have some fun with this rooster, so he trained it to sit on his arm, and he made a little hood for it, the kind falconers put on their falcons when they don't want them flying off. He spent a lot of time with that rooster and finally had it trained the way he wanted. Then he trimmed its feathers to make it look sleeker.

His friends knew what he was up to, and next time there was a cattle sale in town, Vuiko Yurko told them he was going to have some fun with the city guys who always came to these things so they could feel superior to the farmers.

At the sale, there were lots of people from all over the district and everywhere. Lots of cattle, and lots of buyers who came in from all over. It was like a fair, except it was mainly for buying and selling cattle, not having fun.

Anyhow, Vuiko Yurko showed up with this rooster on his arm. It had the hood on its head, and a leather strap tied from its leg to Vuiko Yurko's arm. Just like in the movies, except it wasn't a falcon. Vuiko Yurko figured that some of those city guys wouldn't know the difference.

Pretty soon there was a good-sized crowd gathered around, waiting to see what would happen. Most of the people there knew what a rooster looked like, but they had never seen one sitting on someone's arm before. Vuiko Yurko was talking to some of his friends and everybody was having fun, and then this city guy came up to the crowd.

"They say there's a hunting falcon here," he said, elbowing his way in. "I've always wanted to have a good one, and I'd like to see this bird."

It was time for the fun to begin. Vuiko Yurko went up to the guy, with the rooster.

"This isn't a common, ordinary falcon," he said. "This is a specially-trained hunting bird."

Vuiko Yurko took the hood off the rooster, and the bird shook his head and blinked until he was used to the light. He didn't mind the crowd, because he was with his best pal, Vuiko Yurko.

Vuiko Yurko went to a clear space in the field, with everybody following behind. He took a little rubber ball out of his pocket and put it in the bird's mouth. Then he untied the rooster's leg and whispered in its ear. He took the ball from the rooster and threw it a little way in front of him; the rooster flapped after the ball and came running back to Vuiko Yurko with it.

Well, this was pretty amazing stuff, and everybody started clapping and laughing. The city guy looked pretty excited and was about to say something, when the rooster all of a sudden rared back and crowed real loud, like roosters do. Well, the whole thing was over right there.

The city guy stopped dead in his tracks and stared at the bird. "You know," he started to say, "I kind of thought that something wasn't quite right about that falcon..."

Everybody was laughing by now. Finally, he started to laugh himself. He was the kind of a guy who could take a joke.

Even though Vuiko Yurko didn't quite get away with his little scheme, everybody was still pretty impressed with what he and the rooster had done. After that, every time there was a fair or something, Vuiko Yurko had to take his "falcon" along and give a show. He liked doing that, and the rooster didn't mind, either.

Typical prairie barn and typical Model T.
In doorway: Dido Vasyl Evanishen and sons
John and Peter.

Fixing Cars

Vuiko Yurko had a few old cars in his time. He never owned a new car and he never wanted to, because he had heard that a new car loses a third of its value as soon as you drive it off the lot. I guess that means that it becomes a used car right away and then it's not worth as much. Or something like that. Anyhow, Vuiko Yurko had lots of old cars.

His favorite was always Studebaker. He thought that they were better-designed and better-built than any other cars, and he never passed up a chance to get hold of one.

Sometimes he got a pretty good deal, but sometimes he had to put a lot of work into whatever he bought, just to make it run. It's a good thing he knew how to do stuff like that.

One time, he bought a car from a friend of his who lived a few miles away. He knew the car didn't run, so he got a big rope and jumped in the truck with a few of his friends who just happened to be visiting. They went to where the car was and tied it onto the back of the truck and then drove off. Vuiko Yurko and one of his friends were in the car, and the other two were in the truck, towing.

Since it was Vuiko Yurko's car, he was steering, and his friend was just along for the ride. The guys in the truck were having some kind of a difference of opinion at that particular time, and as soon as they got into the truck and drove off, they were after each other. Of course, each had his mind made up and nobody was going to change it, but it's fun arguing anyway.

When they got to Vuiko Yurko's farm, there was Dotsia in the yard. They stopped the truck and hollered, "Hey Dotsia! What do you think of Vuiko Yurko's new car?"

She looked at them like they were crazy, then went around to the back of the truck and laughed. "It isn't very big, is it?" she said.

They got out of the truck and turned beet red. No car. The rope had come untied some- where along the line, and they had been too busy arguing to notice. Of course, the car had no horn, so Vuiko Yurko couldn't do anything but sit in the middle of the road and hope the Mountie didn't show up before the truck did.

Another time, Vuiko Yurko was going to buy a car from a friend of his and the two of them were out test-driving it. This friend of Vuiko Yurko's was a real back-seat driver, and he kept criticizing Vuiko Yurko's driving until Vuiko Yurko got mad. He pulled on the steering wheel as if to give it to him and hollered, "If you don't like the way I drive, then you do it!" Imagine his surprise when the steering wheel came right off in his hands! They barely got stopped before they drove in the ditch.

Another car Vuiko Yurko bought was in almost perfect shape. He hadn't had it for very long when he decided to take it for a spin one Sunday. They were going to go to the lake for a picnic so he could show off his nice car. He and Dotsia piled everybody and the lunch into the car and set off.

On the way, they had to pass their neighbor's farm, and this neighbor had an ornery bull that kept getting loose. Of course, on this day the bull had to be loose. There it was, in the middle of the road, surrounded by cows. They had busted down the fence somewhere and were just standing there, looking around.

Vuiko Yurko honked the horn and hollered at the bull, but he sure wasn't going to get out of the car to try to move it. So he honked and hollered, but the bull didn't even look at him.

Finally, Vuiko Yurko got mad. He put the car in gear and drove up to it real slow. He was going to push that stupid bull out of the way, and get going to the lake.

Well, pushing the bull was the last thing to do. That bull, as soon as he felt the car pushing on his behind, rared up and started kicking like crazy. This took Vuiko Yurko totally by surprise, and both headlights were busted out before he realized that he had better get out of there.

He put the car in reverse and started backing up, but the kids started hollering right away, "Look out! Here comes the bull!"

That crazy bull was chasing the car. Vuiko Yurko didn't turn around to look, but he put his foot down and made that car go as fast as he could backwards. He didn't want to drive through his neighbor's fence, that was for sure. The bull just kept charging, and Vuiko Yurko just kept driving. Suddenly, as he came over the top of the hill, Vuiko Yurko could see a big old grain truck lumbering up the road.

The road was only wide enough for one car, and there were big sand banks on either side, so all Vuiko Yurko could do was stop the car and hope for the best. The bull didn't stop, though. He was charging with his head down, and he just plowed right into the front of the car. The car bounced back and so did the bull.

When it was all over and the bull finally wandered away down the road, Vuiko Yurko got out to inspect the damage. Broken headlights, smashed grill, hole in radiator. He talked the farmer in the grain truck into towing his nice new car home, and instead of going to the lake to show off, Vuiko Yurko spent the rest of that day trying to put his car back on the road.

Baba Evanishen, John, Dido Vasyl and Peter in front.

Playing with Helicopters

Vuiko Yurko had a furnace in his new house. It was still one of the kind that burned wood and coal, but it was one of those new-fangled things that worked with a thermostat. All you had to do was fill the hopper with coal and then set the thermostat for however hot you wanted it and it ran all day long.

To get the heat from the furnace in the basement to the rest of the house, there was a big metal grate in the floor just above the furnace. There was a hole for the heat and the grate was there so that nobody fell into the basement. The grate was a pretty elaborate affair. It was about three feet across and it was made out of iron. It was real fancy, with flowers and curlicues and stuff all over it.

One day, Vuiko Yurko and Dotsia weren't home. The only one home was Andriy, one of their grandchildren, who was visiting. He was about twelve years old, and a good boy. He was pretty bright, but he was still a kid, and you know how kids are.

Anyhow, this one day he was the only one home. He was waiting for his friend Clinton to come over so they could play. They were always thinking up something to do. As a matter of fact, the only complaint Vuiko Yurko had about his grandchildren was that sometimes they were too noisy when they were building stuff in the basement. They were always making something.

So this one day, Clinton had a book about helicopters. Both boys read it through and then decided that they should make their own. First, they had to do some research and some experimenting so that they knew how the thing worked. They knew that it had something to do with the big fan-thing that turned around on top of the helicopter.

The engine made the rotor, which is what they call the fan-thing, turn. When it turned, it did something with the air, and that made it go up. To test their theories, the boys made some simple helicopters out of paper, like the book said to do.

What you do is take a flat piece of paper and cut a rectangle out of it maybe three or four inches long and one or two inches wide. You cut a slit in it lengthwise about halfway to make the rotor, spread the slit parts, fold up the other end a little for weight, and there you are. By changing the angle of the slit parts, you change the way the rotor makes the thing act. You drop it from as high as you can reach and it spins around like the seeds from a maple tree. Those seeds are organic helicopters.

So the boys made a few of these things and when they dropped them, they spun around and floated down and it was a lot of fun. Pretty soon though, they wanted their helicopters to float longer. They couldn't reach too high, so they got up on chairs and then put a chair on the table and dropped them. More leads to more, and pretty soon they thought they'd go and throw them off the roof of the house.

They went outside, but it was too cold and the wind was blowing too hard, so they went back inside. They were chilly, so they stood on the grate to warm up. While they were discussing their problem, Andriy dropped one of his helicopters. It fell a little way, but the hot air from the furnace made it spin pretty good.

Great ideas are often born from accidents, and that was what happened here. The boys looked at each other, and you could hear their minds go "Click!" They ran to the thermostat, cranked it up to Hot and set about flying their helicopters over the grate.

They set the angles of the rotor and then dropped a helicopter right over the grate. There was enough hot air coming up that they could almost keep the helicopter hovering. They spent hours twisting rotors and changing angles, and trying it again and again until they had a couple of them almost floating on the hot air.

Now and then, they had the angle set completely wrong and a helicopter would fall right down through the grate onto the hot furnace. Then they'd look through the grate and see the paper sitting there smoking and getting brown. Finally, there would be a little puff of flame and the black bits of ash would come floating back up through the grate. It was fun, but it sure didn't smell too good.

Finally, they had one set just exactly right, and the furnace was roaring and sending up a strong enough current so that their helicopter was hovering directly above the grate, all by itself. They sat back and watched it whirling in mid-air, twirling and spinning and neither falling nor rising. Success at last!

Vuiko Yurko and Dotsia picked this moment of triumph to come home. They opened the door to the house and jumped back two feet when they were hit by the blast of hot air. That furnace had been going full bore for a couple of hours and it was pretty hot in there. The boys were too busy to notice, but Dotsia was awful unhappy about all her house plants, which were looking kind of wilted.

"And how about the cat?" hollered Vuiko Yurko. The poor cat was sitting on the floor with its tongue hanging out. It was puffing and panting to beat the band. Dotsia picked it up and put it outside and it looked a little happier.

The plants and the cat recovered, and the boys had to refill the furnace hopper, but they didn't do any more helicopters again that year. With the stinging of their backsides, they learned how dangerous they can be.

Nauka School, near Hafford, Saskatchewan. Note cabooses, sleigh, flagpole and well in yard.

The Hen House

On a farm, there's always a problem trying to keep chickens from getting eaten by wild animals. Since the wild animals were there first, and this new source of food suddenly appeared, you can't blame them from trying to cash in.

The farmer's solution to the wild animal problem was not simply to kill all of them, because that would have been impossible. Plus, they were very often useful to the farmers. For example, it was not uncommon in the winter to go into someone's wood shed and see a whole stack of frozen rabbits piled up like firewood. You caught them whenever you could and stacked them up for when you needed food. Also, furs brought in much-needed cash.

So what the farmer had to do was not eliminate all the wild animals, but keep his chickens away from them. Vuiko Yurko always liked chickens, so he always took good care of his. He not only made sure they were safe; he made sure they were comfortable and happy. He kept them well-fed and watered and there was always at least one rooster around for company.

At first, the chickens stayed in the house with Vuiko Yurko and Dotsia. That was their first house, the dugout in the hill, before they had time to build a hen house. Dotsia was happy when they finally built the hen house, because then she didn't have to clean up after the chickens. She never much liked doing that.

Vuiko Yurko built a nice hen house when he finally got the time. He made it out of wood that was left over from building the barn, and he made it big enough for all the chickens he had and the ones he knew were to come. It was a pretty big place, bigger than some peoples' first houses. There was a row of nice nesting boxes and roosts and a grain dish inside for when it was raining. Then he could feed them inside and they wouldn't get wet.

Most of the time, the chickens went wherever they wanted to. Range-type chickens they were. That meant that Vuiko Yurko didn't have to give them too much grain. They just went out and found whatever they needed. For water, there was a big dish, and a spout that came off the roof of the hen house. When it rained, the water went down the spout and kept the dish full. That meant that when it rained, you didn't have to carry water.

The hen house was pretty strong. It was made of posts with walls of boards nailed together, and the spaces between the boards were filled with moss. There was no insulation, because in those days nobody had even heard of such stuff. Besides, chickens can fluff out their feathers, so they're already insulated.

The hen house was beside the barn, not too far away from the house. It was easy enough to get to, and close enough that if there was a commotion in there, you could hear it from wherever you were on the farm. At first, there was no problem at all. The hen house was strong and safe from any animals.

As time went on, though, the wood at the bottom of the walls of the hen house got kind of rotten, and little holes started to appear. At first it was just mice that would get in to eat the grain, but then the holes got bigger, and Vuiko Yurko got worried that foxes or something would get in. He was waiting for seeding to be over, and then he was going to fix up all those holes.

Before he could get to it, though, he had a disaster. One night, he was in bed and he heard a great squawking and screaming coming from the hen house. Something was in there scaring them.

Vuiko Yurko sprang into action. He always wore his long johns to bed, so he was already dressed in case something like this happened. You know the kind — they're usually red and they go all the way to your feet and your hands and they have a big flap in the back for access.

Anyway, Vuiko Yurko jumped into his boots, grabbed his shotgun on the way out the door, and ran over to the hen house with the flap of his long johns waving in the breeze. He opened the door and bent over so that the moonlight would go in and he could see what was in there. He had hardly opened the door and bent over when his dog came running up. It had been fast asleep and only now woke up.

The dog went running for the hen house, but it didn't see Vuiko Yurko bent over in the doorway, and it ran its cold wet nose right onto Vuiko Yurko's bare back end. Well, that startled Vuiko Yurko so bad that he fired off his shotgun. There was a big Boom! and a bright flash of light added to the squawking and screaming, and now there was a barking and a yelling, too.

As Vuiko Yurko turned around to holler at the dog, he felt something furry streak past his leg. By the time it was all sorted out and Vuiko Yurko had his lantern there, things were a lot quieter, but now he could see how much damage had been done. The shotgun blast had killed three chickens and made a big hole in the wall of the hen house. And the skunk got clean away.

Motorcycles

Motorcycles used to be not so common as they are nowadays. Of course, cars used to be pretty rare, too, but now they're everywhere. Lots of stuff like that is just taken for granted nowadays; in the old days all you could ever take for granted was that you were going to have weather tomorrow. The only thing was, you didn't know what kind of weather.

Anyhow, Vuiko Yurko had a motorcycle or two. They were kind of fun, once you got used to the idea that you weren't allowed to make any mistakes when you were driving them. In a car, you can make all kinds of mistakes and still be alive, but with a motorcycle, it's different. One mistake and it could be all over.

There were so many accidents involving people who weren't used to them that some guys even started called them "Murdercycles."

The first motorcycle Vuiko Yurko had was one of those real old ones with a belt instead of a chain or a shaft, and it didn't have any kind of a starter at all. To get it going, you turned a switch and then pushed as fast as you could. When it fired, you jumped on and away you went.

One time, Vuiko Yurko was going to give a ride to a friend of his who had never been on a motorcycle before. He explained the starting system, and then got things ready. It was easier with two people, because you could sit on the motorcycle and the other guy could push you. Then, when it started, he would jump on.

So this time, Vuiko Yurko sat on the motorcycle and turned it on. His friend pushed a bit and then jumped on. Nothing. Vuiko Yurko then had to explain a little bit about the noise of the motor. If you don't hear that noise, then the motor isn't going.

Okay, try again. This time his friend pushed like crazy, and the motor started. Unfortunately, Vuiko Yurko had the throttle opened a bit too much, and when the thing started, it just zoomed straight forward. When his friend jumped for the seat, the motorcycle shot right out from under him and he leaped into thin air and landed in the road on the seat of his pants. That was enough motorcycle riding for him. He walked home.

Another time Vuiko Yurko was going to go for a ride. He got everything ready and pushed the machine real hard. It didn't want to go, so he pushed and pushed and pushed. Finally, he did a bit of adjusting on the carburetor and tried again. This time it started, but whatever he had done to the carburetor was the wrong thing.

The motorcycle took off all by itself. It ripped its handlebars out of his hands and just sped away. He stood there and thought some strange and dark thoughts, and then the thing caught a clump of dirt and changed direction. Now it was heading right for him! He jumped up onto the hay wagon and watched that mad bike bounce off his car and fall down.

This was even worse. Now the machine was on its side, roaring full blast, going in circles and spraying gravel all over the yard. Finally, it bumped up against a post and stopped moving. It was still screaming full bore, but now at least Vuiko Yurko could get near it and do something about it. He didn't have that thing much longer.

Vuiko Yurko's daughter Sonia once was going out with a guy who had a motorcycle. He came to visit her one day, and they spent a pleasant time together. When it came time for him to leave, he fired up his motorcycle and started to drive away. He was looking behind at Sonia, and when he turned around, he saw that he was heading right for the sand box where Sonia's little cousin was playing.

He swerved and hit a rut at the same time. The result was that he lost control and plowed straight into the hay wagon that was sitting there. He hit it so hard he broke two spokes of the wagon wheel. He was lucky that he didn't get hurt himself. Just a bruise or two. Of course, the motorcycle was bent, and so was his pride.

Vuiko Yurko heard the noise and came out to see what was going on. He took in the scene at a glance and then, shaking his head sadly, said, "Such a big country, such a big yard, and still it's not big enough."

Vuiko Yurko had some old motorcycles like this.

The New Lawn

In the first house Vuiko Yurko built, there were no luxuries. Not even a door; he used an old blanket, and a moose took even that. But that's another story. In the next house there were windows and doors and everything. By the third house there was even a floor, a real floor, not just packed earth.

As time went by and Vuiko Yurko got better off, his and Dotsia's wants increased. Their needs were always the same, but their wants increased. And so it happened that when the newest house ("Our last house!") was being built, Dotsia decided that she wanted a lawn.

There weren't many lawns in the district at that time. Oh sure, there was grass a-plenty, but nobody had a proper lawn that you could sit on without getting dirt on your bottom. Well, even Vuiko Yurko got excited. He had to have a lawn.

He bought some bags of grass seed and some books and he began to read about how to do it.

The first thing was to get the area ready. That wasn't too difficult. The house was already built on a pretty flat place, so he just leveled it off a little more with the tractor and then spread a bit of topsoil around on the ground.

It was sure easy working with the tractor. Not like doing it all by hand. Since this was going to be a pretty big lawn, it had to be done by machine. Vuiko Yurko got everything ready and then told the kids to fill the seeder with the bags from the shed while he did something else. They did that and he went and seeded the whole lawn. Then he watered it and waited and watched.

According to what he had read, the grass should come up pretty soon, but he waited a long time and nothing grew but weeds, and they grew real good. He watered the lawn and chased the birds away, but still no grass.

"Maybe it needs fertilizer," he thought, and he went out to his shed to see if he had the right kind. He looked around, but he couldn't find any fertilizer, only all these nice big bags of grass seed. Oh no! Okay, so maybe he didn't tell the kids which bags from the shed to put in the seeder, but they still should have *grumble grumble grumble*...

Well, now the mice had got in and ruined the grass seed and it was getting too late in the season to get more seed and expect it to grow

111

this year. Only one thing to do. In one article he read, they were talking about that turf stuff you can buy to make a lawn. It's like a big thick carpet, but it's really grass with some dirt on it, and it's rolled up and you just unroll it on the ground and it grows and there's your lawn.

There was a place in the city that did that kind of thing. They grew the grass and then cut it up and rolled it up and sold it. They delivered it to you, too. It was more expensive than sowing your own, but it was a lot quicker.

Vuiko Yurko figured he would only do a part of the lawn, and then seed the rest of it again next spring. He wanted a lawn now. He called up the place and told them what he wanted and they came out and delivered the lawn and showed him how to do it. In no time at all, he and the kids had a big plot laid out and watered, and it looked really good. Instant lawn!

Next morning, Vuiko Yurko looked out the window at his nice new lawn and saw that every bit of the turf was all rolled up again! What is this?! He went out and looked at it, and then he went back to the house and hollered at the kids.

"Nice big joke," he said, "but you can put it all back now."

"We didn't do it," they said.

"Well, so who did it?"

"Dunno, but it sure wasn't us. Do you think we'd make all that extra work for ourselves?"

So there was a mystery for them to think about. Maybe some neighbor kids were just having some fun. But what a lot of work just for some fun. They got busy and laid all the turf back down and then watered it again.

Next morning, Vuiko Yurko looked out the window, and there it was all rolled up again. Every piece. This was getting silly. He and the kids unrolled all of it again and watered it again. That night, they were going to sit up with a shotgun and see who was doing this.

They left the yard light on and sat in the kitchen and watched. Nothing happened until it got real dark. Then Vuiko Yurko looked out and saw one piece of turf was rolled up. Now, how did that happen while he was watching? He looked, and saw another piece rolling itself up.

He stood and stared, and then he saw, coming out from behind the roll, a raccoon! He watched the raccoon put its nose under the end of another strip and start to push. It rolled up the turf and then picked up the worms and the grubs that live under such places. So that was it! Hungry raccoons!

Next day, they tied the dogs around the lawn, and that took care of the raccoons until the grass took a good enough hold. Finally, there was a lawn. It looked really good in just a few weeks, with all the care Vuiko Yurko gave it. He was going to take proper care of this lawn. Cut it and fertilize it and rake it and water it. He had read up on it and he knew just what to do.

In the spring, the lawn had to be power-raked. That's to get the matted dead grass away from the roots so that it can breathe. Well, Vuiko Yurko didn't have the rake to do this, and it was too much of a chore for the kids to do it by hand. They were needed other places, anyway. Always lots of work to do on a farm.

Vuiko Yurko knew how his chickens scratched when they were hunting for food, so he thought he could get them to do the raking. He threw some grain out on the lawn and called the chickens. They came running, and didn't they have a field day! They clucked and scratched all day long, and Vuiko Yurko kept throwing grain in the parts that hadn't been done yet, until it was all done.

"They did a good job raking," he said, "and I didn't have to fertilize the lawn that year!"

Vuiko Yurko's Sayings

Vuiko Yurko was a pretty sharp character. His mind was really quick, and so was his tongue. He was such a popular guy that everyone knew him, and everyone had their favorite story about what he had done or what he had said. Here are some of the things he was supposed to have said or done.

For example, someone once asked him how long he had been married. "I don't know," he answered. "When was Christ born?"

When he was asked how he lived to such an old age, he said, "No smoking, no drinking, eat well, sleep well and don't go out after dark."

Once when he had done someone a favor and they said, "Thank you, Vuiko Yurko. I'll do the same for you some day," he said, "Why couldn't you do it right now?"

When someone was saying something to him that he knew was not true, he used to say, "Don't give me that string of line."

Vuiko Yurko picked up English pretty quick, but he liked to tell stories about the funny things people used to say when they were learning. Like the fellow that was explaining to a curling club how the tournament was going to run. "First this team play that team, then that team play that team, then that team play that team. After that, it's eat, dog, eat!"

One of his favorite sayings was "If you go to sleep with dogs, you'll wake up with fleas."

When he first saw one of those skyscrapers in the city, he called it a "cloud-ripper."

Once he was talking about something they used to do when they were young and he said, "They was kids and I was kids."

Vuiko Yurko also liked to tell about the time he was in a small town on the prairies and he was hungry, so he went to the only restaurant in town. When he got there, he found a sign that said "Closed for Lunch."

Vuiko Yurko had some grandchildren who didn't know much Ukrainian, but he thought he would teach them a little song anyway, in Ukrainian. He did that, and the kids learned the song. He never told them what it meant, and they never asked.

Later on, they sang the song for their mother, and she was quite shocked. "Who taught you that?" she asked them. "Dido," they said. "Oh," was all she could say. Here's how the song went in English (of course, it doesn't rhyme very well in English):

> When we were in Old Ukraine
> We were good Cossacks.
> We sat down by the house
> And farted like bulls.

Vuiko Yurko liked to make fun of how much trouble he had learning English. He'd say, "For tree year I learning how to say Gallyoon (gallon) now they changing to Yog (jug)!"

Another one he liked was, "You trash my field, I plow you back."

"If a Holstein is a cow," he once said, "then a calf must be a Halfstein."

One other misunderstanding he liked to tell about was when one of his grandchildren used to refer to "Bedouin" slippers. It turns out that when he was little, the boy heard someone talk about "bedroom" slippers, but he didn't hear it right, and that's how it sounded to him. Later, when he was able to read, he ran across the Bedouin people in a story about Africa, so it all made sense to him. It wasn't until he was an adult that he finally figured out his mistake.

Vuiko Yurko was being mischievous once, and someone accused him of being a "bad boy." "I'm not a bad boy," he said. "I'm an okay man."

When he was talking about a long-winded friend of his, he said, "Oh yeah, and he'll tell you that story as many times as you want to hear it!" Or he'd say, "If you ask him for the time, he'll tell you how to make a clock."

Vuiko Yurko also liked to tell the story of his neighbor who went to Québec and was hauled into court for not stopping at a Stop sign, which there says "Arrêt." The man explained to the judge that he came to the sign, and it said "Awright," so he just kept going.

One time Vuiko Yurko was taking a short-cut across his neighbor's field, and his neighbor, who was an old sourpuss, said, "I'm sorry, but that's not the road." Vuiko Yurko asked him, "Do you know where I'm going?" "No, I do not." "Well then, how do you know it's not the road?"

Once he was reading a letter for a friend of his, and the letter was from some lawyer, who signed his name something like "John Smith, Junior." The friend asked what that Junior after his name meant, and Vuiko Yurko said, "That's to show that he's not as old as his father."

Vuiko Yurko was walking past a field one day, and the farmer there was working on his hay. "Hey, Vuiko Yurko," he called. "Is this fine weather going to keep up all day?" "I don't know," Vuiko Yurko said, "but I'm coming back this way tonight, and I'll tell you then."

Vuiko Yurko was driving a pig along the road one day when some smart-aleck boys saw him go by. "Hey, Vuiko Yurko!" one of them called out, "Is that your brother?" "No," he replied, "just a friend, the same as you."

One more story Vuiko Yurko liked to tell about one of his neighbors. The neighbor had had a sick cow some time before, and one of his friends came to him and said, "What did you give your sick cow?" The neighbor said, "I gave her a quart of linseed oil." Two days later, the friend saw the neighbor and told him, "I did like you said and I gave my sick cow a quart of linseed oil, and she died." "I'm not surprised," said the neighbor. "So did mine."

Stan's Lunch Bar in Krydor, Saskatchewan.
Stan's was never Closed for Lunch.

The Sermon in the House

Back in the old days before they had kids, Vuiko Yurko and Dotsia lived in a little one-room house that they had built for themselves. It was comfortable enough for the two of them, but there sure wasn't any room left over.

While Vuiko Yurko did most of the work in the field, Dotsia took care of the house and the garden and the chickens. They always had chickens. When they first got their chickens, they weren't quite ready for them, though.

A neighbor was leaving the district and he wanted to get rid of his livestock, so Vuiko Yurko bought his chickens. He took them home and let them loose in the yard, then went back to his field. Later, he and Dotsia began to figure out how they could keep the chickens safe.

"If we leave them outside, they're sure to be grabbed by a wild animal."

"How about building a hen house?"

"Right now there's no time. The field has to be got ready for planting."

"Well, what else can we do?"

Finally, they agreed that the only thing they could do was keep the chickens in the house at night. They cleared out a corner and made a roost, and the chickens slept there. Every morning Dotsia shooed them out and cleaned up their mess, and everything was okay. The only problem was that the chickens liked to go into the house during the day. Mostly this was okay, but one time it was sort of embarrassing.

In those days, there weren't many priests or ministers in the countryside, so whenever one showed up, you dropped what you were doing and called all the neighbors and had a service. Sometimes it was months before you could do a proper baptism or anything.

One day, a priest showed up at Vuiko Yurko's house, just out of the blue. Dotsia came out of the garden and made him at home, and then ran to Vuiko Yurko to tell him the news. He ran to the neighbor's place to tell him that they were going to have a service that afternoon, as the priest was just passing by. The neighbor and his family also dropped everything and went with Vuiko Yurko.

The priest was a young fellow who hadn't done much preaching, but he had everything properly set up in the little house. When everybody was inside he started the service and everything was just fine. When he got to his sermon, however, he started getting nervous again. He had just written it while he was on the road, and he wasn't used to it yet.

He was actually going along pretty good until he reached the part in his sermon where he was talking about "the beasts of the earth and the fowls of the air." Suddenly, there was a tremendous squawking and gabbling going on right under the table he was using for an altar.

Two chickens had been sleeping under the table, and he had stepped on one, and that woke up the both of them and they bounced around squawking and strewing feathers all over the place and raising such a dust and a ruckus! The poor priest had been startled half out of his wits.

When the chickens were finally chased out and the service was over, everyone went outside. The priest was especially relieved. He received all kinds of compliments on his sermon, though, and everybody said it had been one of the most exciting they had ever heard.

The Shopkeeper

Vuiko Yurko ran a general store for a few years. He used to be a farmer, but he thought he would try something different when this store came up for sale, and he bought it. He sold all kinds of things in that store, like you had to in a small community. There was only one store and everyone shopped there.

Vuiko Yurko was as fair about everything as he could be. Sometimes it was hard trying to explain that he had to make a profit on everything he sold, or he would go out of business and then people would have to drive miles to get to another store. And he couldn't do much about the price he paid for his goods. But he was a fair man to begin with, so he did okay.

Since people didn't understand business, or even if they did, they used to poke fun at all shopkeepers. Sometimes it wasn't so much in fun, but to get their frustration out of their system, they used to pick on the owners of the stores. They called them bad names sometimes and told mean jokes about them. They used to say about any store owner: "He's a good man. He would give you the shirt off your back."

Vuiko Yurko had some funny experiences at his store. One time, there was a young boy in the shop who wanted to buy something that he really wanted, but he didn't have enough money. Vuiko Yurko knew the boy and his parents, who were fairly well off, and the boy had lots of other toys and things, so he said to the boy, "I'm sorry you don't have enough money, but you should be content with what you have."

"I am content with what I have," said the boy. "It's what I don't have that I'm sad about."

Another time a farmer came in and couldn't remember what it was his wife had asked him to buy. He sat by the stove and wracked his brains and thought and thought and just couldn't come up with it. Vuiko Yurko tried to help, but there were other customers to take care of, and he wasn't all that much help.

Finally, the man looked up and spotted the priest in the store. His face all of a sudden brightened up and he jumped to his feet and hollered, "Father, what's that other name they call the Devil?"

"You mean Satan?"

"Yah! That's it! Vuiko Yurko, give me one yard of that Satan for my wife so she can finish making her dress!"

Once, one of Vuiko Yurko's buddies was sitting by the stove and there were people in the store and Vuiko Yurko was busy. He saw a woman steal a shirt and stuff it in her bag. He saw that Vuiko Yurko had watched her do this.

After she had left, the man said to Vuiko Yurko, "You saw that woman take that shirt. Why didn't you do anything about it?"

"If I had made a fuss about it," said Vuiko Yurko, "she and her whole family would never come in here again. I can't afford to lose their business, so I let her take it. But I know how much it cost, and she'll pay for it. I'll just add a little onto each of her bills until it's covered. And because she's so dishonest, she will pay double."

One day when Vuiko Yurko and his cronies were sitting around on their chairs in front of his store and nobody was in the store, they heard a great ruckus coming from around the corner. It sounded like some people were hollering at each other and a big fight was about to break out.

Everybody jumped up and rushed around the corner to see what was going on, and there they found two old farmers who they knew were both hard of hearing. The two guys were having themselves a conversation about the weather and their crops, but they both had to holler so loud that it sounded like a pitched battle.

Vuiko Yurko served most of the customers himself, and he knew most of them. One day, though, he was rummaging around with his head under the counter, and he heard someone say, "How much are your apples today?"

"Ten cents," he said with his head still under the counter. Then, when he looked up, he saw he was talking to a total stranger.

"Oops! I mean fifteen cents!"

The stranger just laughed. He used to have a store too, and he knew that if you could get away with it, you charged strangers and tourists more than you did the local people. When he started to laugh, Vuiko Yurko knew that he had been caught, so he started to laugh, too. They finally settled on twelve cents for the apple.

Another time, a stranger came in and bought a couple of things. Then he asked for a box of fancy biscuits he saw on the shelf, the last package of those biscuits. Vuiko Yurko took the box down and the man opened it to have one. Imagine his surprise when he found the box was empty! Not one biscuit in it.

"Hey, what's this?" he said.

Vuiko Yurko took the box from him and looked at it and, sure enough, it was empty. Well, what is this? He turned the box over and found that the bottom had been torn open and then glued shut again.

"Those kids! Wait till I get to them!" shouted Vuiko Yurko. He knew what had happened. His kids had been in the store one day and decided to have themselves a little secret treat. This time they didn't get away with it.

It was hard to get good help, then, just like now and just like always. Times were tough and people would try to find any kind of a job, just so they could eat. Vuiko Yurko needed someone to help him run the store, so he let people know that he was looking for someone.

One day, this young man came to the store. Vuiko Yurko knew him, and he knew that he was a good boy, but he thought just a bit too much of himself. He had gone to the city to school, after all.

"Okay," said Vuiko Yurko, "we'll give you a try. Here's what you do. First thing in the morning before we open, you sweep the floor..."

"Sweep the floor!" exclaimed the boy. "But I'm a university graduate!"

"Oh, that's okay," replied Vuiko Yurko, "I'll show you how to do it!"

The Christmas Concert

Vuiko Yurko lived near a village made up of mostly Ukrainian people and, every Christmas, there was always a concert put on by the schools and the churches and the Ukrainian reading societies and whoever else was interested. It was the social event of the year as far as the whole district was concerned.

Vuiko Yurko didn't actually take part in many of these concerts, but he was always there to help if they needed him. He didn't feel too good about getting up on stage in front of lots of people, but he liked to help backstage.

So this one year, there's a concert coming and Vuiko Yurko is helping out. He's making some stuff for the actors to use in the play and painting some sets and things like that. He was always good at that kind of thing.

The rehearsals are going along like they usually do. Some of the people know their parts and others don't have a clue what they're supposed to be doing. Just like usual. Kids running all over the place. Also just like usual.

One rehearsal day, pretty close to the performance, things still aren't quite coming together. Everybody's getting scared because they're not ready. It's time for the rehearsal to start, but the director isn't there. Somebody comes in and says he's sick.

So now what? Nobody's ready and the director is sick. Everybody just kind of sits there, and some kids start to cry because they've worked so hard for so long and now all that work is wasted and so on and so on.

It's looking so bad that Vuiko Yurko finally stands up and says, "Okay, do you want a concert or don't you?"

It's quiet then and somebody says, "Well, sure we do, but we're not ready and there's not much time and now we don't have a director."

"Okay," says Vuiko Yurko. "You need a director, I'll be your director. But you all have to do exactly what I tell you."

Everybody looks at everybody else. How is this going to work out? Nobody has ever seen Vuiko Yurko do anything like this before. Well, okay, let's try it. Why not?

"I'll do it just this one time," he says, "and you all behave and do what I say."

Then he starts giving everybody orders: Tania, do this; Eugene, do this; Myron, do that; Marianna, do that.

Some of them are starting to get ready, but a couple of others are still kind of hysterical, so Vuiko Yurko takes them aside and talks to them and then everybody gets right to work. In no time at all, everyone's busy doing something and they all feel a lot better.

That night at rehearsal, there's a big difference in how they feel about the concert. Before, they were kind of worried that it might not work out, but now that somebody like Vuiko Yurko is in charge and yelling around the place, everybody feels a lot better.

The concert is going to be held pretty soon, and in between, there's a whole lot of work being done. The sets have to be finished and they are, even though the paint is still wet when the curtain goes up. The costumes and the lights and the makeup and the tickets and the chairs and wood for the stove and everything is done. The music for the dancers is ready and everything. Vuiko Yurko made sure it was done.

The night of the concert, there's all the last-minute stuff to be done, like there always is. Somebody's ribbons fell off and somebody else can't find their bottle of horse liniment for the play and one of the sets falls over and gets paint on somebody's shirt. Business as usual.

Finally, it's time for the curtain to go up. By that, I mean it's half an hour after the time it was supposed to start. Things backstage are still pretty hectic. Everybody's so busy that nobody notices the Master of Ceremonies, who is sitting in a corner with his program, and he's just sitting there reading it over and over. He's nervous.

He's so nervous that every now and then he takes a little bottle out of his pocket and has a sip. Maybe it's the lost horse liniment. Nope. It's his own stuff. By the time the concert is ready to start, he's asleep in his corner.

Now it's time to start. Vuiko Yurko goes to him and says, "Okay, let's go."

Nothing. He's asleep and he smells like a home brew barrel. There's a little bit of a panic then, because nobody else can be the Master of Ceremonies, since nobody else knows the whole show. They only know their own parts. Vuiko Yurko is the director; he has to do it.

Well, Vuiko Yurko doesn't much like being up in front of everybody, but he figures maybe it's sort of like being a witness in court, when you're sitting in the box and everybody's looking at you. That's not too bad. Okay, he'll do it.

He grabs the program from the body of the old MC and tries to remember how it's all done. He peeks out past the curtain like the kids have been doing all night, and he sees the hall is packed. Every seat is filled and people are standing at the back and it's hot and steamy in there and kids are running around and everybody's having a great time talking with their neighbors. Then somebody sees Vuiko Yurko's face poking through the curtains.

"Hey Vuiko Yurko! Let's get going!"

So now he has to do it. Okay, don't be nervous, do like you've seen them do it before. It's mostly in Ukrainian, except for the names of some of the music the performers are going to play, so that much is easy. He steps out in front of the curtain and looks around.

"Good evening," says Vuiko Yurko, and the hall goes quiet. Nobody knew he was going to do this. So Vuiko Yurko digs into his memory and does like he's seen it done a hundred times.

First, he apologizes for the show starting late. Everybody does that. Then he apologizes for the paint being still wet on some of the sets. And then he says sorry for this and sorry for that, and he winds up apologizing for the whole wonderful show which is to follow.

Then he starts to tell a joke, like you're supposed to. Some joke like: "When my father came to this country, he saw a sign that said Drink Canada Dry." But Vuiko Yurko is too nervous and he stumbles over the punch line, but it doesn't matter, because everybody knows the joke and the whole audience roars out together, "And he's still trying!"

Of course, this is a lot of fun and it makes everybody relax and the evening gets into full swing and everybody has a marvellous time.

Every Ukrainian Christmas concert
featured dancers in costumes similar to these.
Photo taken in Meadow Lake, Saskatchewan.

In this glossary:

[a] is pronounced as in f<u>a</u>r
[e] is pronounced as in g<u>e</u>t
[ee] is pronounced as in f<u>ee</u>t
[i] is pronounced as in s<u>i</u>t
[o] is pronounced as between g<u>o</u>t and g<u>oa</u>t
[oo] is pronounced as in l<u>oo</u>se
[y] is pronounced as in <u>y</u>es